D0938676

CONTEMPORARY BRITISH DRAMA 1950–1976

Also by E. H. Mikhail

The Social and Cultural Setting of the 1890s
John Galsworthy the Dramatist
Comedy and Tragedy
Sean O'Casey: A Bibliography of Criticism
A Bibliography of Modern Irish Drama 1899–1970
Dissertations on Anglo-Irish Drama: A Bibliography of Studies 1870–1970
The Sting and the Twinkle: Conversations with Sean O'Casey *(co-editor with John O'Riordan)*
J. M. Synge: A Bibliography of Criticism
J. M. Synge: Interviews and Recollections *(editor)*
W. B. Yeats: Interviews and Recollections (two volumes) *(editor)*
British Drama 1900–1950
Lady Gregory: Interviews and Recollections *(editor)*
Oscar Wilde: An Annotated Bibliography
Oscar Wilde: Interviews and Recollections (two volumes) *(editor)*
Contemporary British Drama 1950–1976
A Research Guide to Modern Irish Dramatists
Brendan Behan: An Annotated Bibliography of Criticism

CONTEMPORARY BRITISH DRAMA 1950–1976

An Annotated Critical Bibliography

E. H. MIKHAIL

With a foreword by
William A. Armstrong

First edition 1976
Reprinted 1979

Published by
THE MACMILLAN PRESS LTD
London and Basingstoke

Associated companies in Delhi Dublin Hong Kong Johannesburg Lagos Melbourne New York Singapore Tokyo

ISBN 0 333 19913 8

Printed in Great Britain by
BILLING & SONS LTD
Guildford, Worcester, and London

Contents

Foreword

Professor Edward H. Mikhail needs no introduction to students and general readers of twentieth-century drama; he is already well known for his book on John Galsworthy and his bibliographical guides to modern Irish drama (1972), Sean O'Casey (1972), dissertations on Anglo-Irish drama (1973) and J. M. Synge (1975). The bibliography offered in the present volume has the salient virtues that we have come to associate with him: aptness of arrangement, thoroughness of coverage, accuracy of detail, and a truly admirable capacity for pithy and discerning comments on the content and argument of the books that he has listed.

The last merit is a particularly valuable feature of the present work, for it covers an exceptionally wide range of topics, and here perhaps, a few words of introduction will not come amiss. The development of British Drama during the past twenty-five years has been a fascinating but complex phenomenon. The idealistic verse drama of the postwar decade was elbowed aside by the caustic and iconoclastic young playwrights headed by John Osborne in the later 1950s, and their trenchant activities have been followed by the so-called New Movement, which is still in progress and has experimented with various themes and techniques for which critics have tried to find more or less accurate lables–Theatre of the Absurd, Theatre of Protest, Theatre of Menace, Theatre of Cruelty, Compressionist Drama, Black Comedy, Documentary Drama, Theatre of Nudity, Theatre of Hope. This variety of experiment has been possible largely because of unprecedented public subsidies for theatres in London and the provinces provided by the Arts Council and

Local Authorities. The institution of a National Theatre and the abolition of the censorship of plays also occurred during this period. So did the establishment of a number of Departments in Drama in British universities. Experimental productions in little 'fringe' theatres and lunch-time performances in small theatres and public houses have become a regular practice. Since 1950, drama has been argued about and written about more than any other art in Britain.

All these developments are welcome signs of life and growth. But serious tensions, excesses and problems have also emerged during the past quarter of a century. Iconoclasm and innovation have sometimes become ends in themselves; producers of Shakespeare's plays have frequently ignored his intentions and mangled his texts to make them fit topical moulds. The importance of the dramatist's text and the spoken word in drama have been challenged, often with dubious results, by devotees of improvisation and mimetic action. In provincial repertory theatres there have been vitiating conflicts between avant garde producers and their boards of management and local audiences. Television drama has become a serious counter-attraction to the live theatre, offering larger rewards and commanding a far bigger audience. Steeply rising costs of production in the live theatre have led to an increase in the price of seats and urgent demands for additional subsidies at a time when inflation is rampant. The completion of the National Theatre has been seriously delayed.

The outstanding merit of Professor Mikhail's bibliography is that it provides clear guidance to every aspect of this diversity of developments. It includes books and articles by British, American and Western European writers, and also Russian, Hungarian, Romanian and Japanese publications. It makes it easy for the reader to study the pros and cons of the new theories and practices of the younger playwrights, of the claims of the best television drama to be a new and independent art, of the belief that the Theatres Act of 1968 has made the dramatist 'the most carefully protected of all public performers' by abolishing censorship. It shows that German critics have been keenly interested in assessing the nature of Brecht's influence on British dramatists, and that Americans have been continuously shrewd, perceptive and sympathetic observers of theatrical activities in Britain. Professor Mikhail's excellent annotations reveal that one of them, writing in 1958, has argued that 'a common theme of postwar British writers is the death of the past and the need to create a new and living identity which will be seen to be related to the past,' and that another, writing in 1972, has decided that 'no other nation in the world can equal the industry and inventiveness of Britain's living dramatists.' Whether or not this high praise is deserved can be assessed by pondering other entries in Professor Mikhail's bibliography. Whatever we may conclude, there is no doubting our debt to him for this timely, scholarly and comprehensive guide. It makes the appetite grow by what it feeds on.

WILLIAM A. ARMSTRONG

Birkbeck College
University of London

Bibliographics

Abstracts of English Studies, 1958 to the present (Boulder, Colorado: National Council of Teachers of English). Gives summaries of articles in periodicals.

Adelman, Irving and Rita Dworkin *Modern Drama; A Checklist of Critical Literature on 20th Century Plays* (Metuchen, New Jersey: Scarecrow Press, 1967). An index to selective commentaries in books and periodicals on modern playwrights and their plays.

Allen, Charles and Felix Pollak, eds. *Comprehensive Index to English-Language Little Magazines, 1890–1970* (Millwood, New York: Kraus-Thomson, 1975). A bibliography for secondary authors, arranged alphabetically according to contributor.

American Doctoral Dissertations, 1963 to the present. Compiled for the Association of Research Libraries (Ann Arbor, Michigan: University Microfilms). Continuation of *Doctoral Dissertations*.

Annotated Bibliography of New Publications in the Performing Arts, 1973 to the present. A quarterly that catalogues books 'as soon as they become generally available in the United States and England.'

Annual Bibliography of English Language and Literature, 1920 to the present (London: Modern Humanities Research Association). Lists books and articles.

Annual Magazine Subject-Index, 1907–49 (Boston: F. W. Faxon). Reprinted as *Cumulated Magazine Subject Index, 1907–1949* (Boston: G. K. Hall, 1964). Lists articles in periodicals.

Belknap, S. Yancey. *Guide to the Performing Arts*, 1957 to the present (New York: Scarecrow Press, 1958). '. . . the first annual index of the performing arts.' Lists articles in periodicals.

Bell, Inglis F. and Jennifer Gallup. *A Reference Guide to English, American, and Canadian Literature; An Annotated Checklist of Bibliographical and Other Reference Materials* (Vancouver, British Columbia: University of British Columbia Press, 1971).

Besterman, Theodore. 'Drama and Stage,' *A World Bibliography of Bibliographies*, 5 vols, 4th ed. (Lausanne: Societas Bibliographica, 1965–6). Annotated and arranged under general and specific subject matter.

———. *Literature: English & American; A Bibliography of Bibliographies* (Totowa, New Jersey: Rowman and Littlefield, 1971).

———. *Music and Drama: A Bibliography of Bibliographies* (Totowa, New Jersey: Rowman and Littlefield, 1971). Compiled by the publisher from the fourth edition of the author's *A World Bibliography of Bibliographies* and of bibliographical catalogues, calendars, abstracts, digests, indexes, etc.

Bibliographic Index; A Cumulative Bibliography of Bibliographies, 1937 to the present (New York: H. W. Wilson). The standard serial Bibliography of bibliographies.

Biddulph, Helen R. and Julia H. Mailer, comps. *Bibliography of Books, Pamphlets and Magazines Relating to Community Theatre* (New York: AETA, 1966). A mimeographed and stapled pamphlet suggesting some possible sources of information on various theatre subjects related to community theatre.

Bond, Donald F. *A Reference Guide to English Studies*, 2nd ed. (Chicago and London: University of Chicago Press, 1971). '. . . designed primarily for the use of the graduate student.'

Book Review Digest, 1906 to the present (New York: H. W. Wilson). An index to reviews in selected periodicals of books published in the United States. Some excerpts are included.

Book Review Index, 1965 to present (Detroit, Michigan: Gale Research Company). Lists reviews of books in periodicals.

Breed, Paul F. and Florence M. Sniderman, eds. *Dramatic Criticism Index; A Bibliography of Commentaries on Playwrights from Ibsen to the Avant-Garde*, (Detroit, Michigan: Gale Research Company, 1972). Its nearly 12,000 entries attempted to cover the English-language books, chapters and articles relating to each playwright and his works.

British Humanities Index, 1962 to the present (London: Library Association). Continuation of *Subject Index to Periodicals*. Subject and author index.

British Museum Subject Index, 1881 to the present (London: Trustees of the British Museum). Includes a section listing books on 'Drama and Stage: Great Britain and Ireland.'

The British National Bibliography, 1950 to the present (London: Council of the British National Bibliography). 'A Subject Catalogue of new books published in the British Isles . . . classified, with modifications, according to the Dewey Decimal Classification.'

Brockett, Oscar G., Samuel L. Becker and Donald C. Bryant. *A Bibliographical Guide to Research in Speech and Dramatic Art* (Boston: Scott, Foresman, 1963). Lists the important aids and reference tools in the field.

Brown, John Russell. 'English Drama Since 1945,' *English Drama (excluding Shakespeare); Select Bibliographical Guides*, ed. Stanley Wells (London: Oxford University Press, 1975), pp. 290–8. Provides a critical guide to the period as well as a list giving bibliographical information about the writings mentioned in the text.

Busfield, Roger M., ed. *Theatre Arts Publications Available in the United States 1953–1957: A Five Year Bibliography* (New York: AETA, 1964). Oriented toward production, but pp. 80–1 include entries on English drama.

Bush, George E. and Jeanne K. Welcher. 'A Check List of Modern Plays Based on Classical Mythic Themes,' *Bulletin of the New York Public Library,* LXXIII (1969), 525–30. Concerns itself solely with modern dramatic versions of classical myths.

Byrne, M. St Clare, ed. 'Modern,' *British Drama: History and Criticism* (London: National Book League, 1950), pp. 16–18. Gives selected reading on the subject.

Canadian Periodical Index, 1938 to the present (Ottawa: Canadian Library Association). Includes a section on 'Drama.'

Carlson, Marvin. 'Modern Drama: A Selected Bibliography of Bibliographies,' *Modern Drama,* VIII, no. 1 (May 1965), 112–18. Annotated list of bibliographies devoted in whole or part to critical works.

Carpenter, Charles A. 'The New Bibliography of Modern Drama Studies,' *Modern Drama,* XII, no. 1 (May 1969), 49–56. Survey.

———. 'Modern Drama Studies: An Annual Bibliography,' *Modern Drama,* XVII, no. 1 (March 1974), 67–120. '. . . intended as a new, improved version of the old ingroup checklist (by Shedd).'

Cheshire, David. *Theatre: History, Criticism and Reference*, The Readers Guide Series (London: Clive Bingley; Hamden, Connecticut: Archon Books, 1967). Examines principal or significant works.

Chicorel, Marietta, ed. *Chicorel Theater Index to Plays in Collections, Anthologies, Periodicals, and Discs*, 3 vols (New York: Chicorel, 1970–2). Indexes plays, playwrights, editors and play collections.

———, ed. *Chicorel Bibliography to the Performing Arts* (New York: Chicorel, 1972). A buying guide that lists entries under subject headings.

———, ed. *Chicorel Theater Index to Plays in Anthologies, Periodicals, Discs & Tapes: Plays on Discs and Tapes* (New York: Chicorel, 1972). Indexes plays and performers on recorded media.

———. *Chicorel Index to the Spoken Arts on Discs, Tapes and Cassettes* (New York: Chicorel, 1973). Lists plays, novels, short stories, speeches, commentaries, conversations, poems and readings.

Clough, Peter H. 'A Subject Index to *Drama Survey*, 1961–1968,' *Theatre Documentation,* III, nos 1–2 (Fall 1970; Spring 1971), 81–100. A cumulative index arranged under twelve topic areas.

Clunes, Alec. *British Theatre History* (London: National Book League, 1955). Gives a selected reading on the subject for the ordinary reader.

Coleman, Arthur and Gary R. Tyler. *Drama Criticism, Volume One: A Checklist of Interpretation Since 1940 of English and American Plays* (Denver, Colorado: Alan Swallow, 1966). Lists studies of plays written in books and periodicals.

Colley, D. I. *Handlist of Plays* (Manchester: Manchester Public Library, 1965). Lists over 2600 titles in the play collection of the Manchester Public Libraries by author, number of characters and sets.

Comprehensive Dissertation Index 1861–1972, 37 vols (Ann Arbor, Michigan: University Microfilms).

Cumulative Book Index, 1928 to the present (New York: H. W. Wilson). A world list of books in the English language.

Descriptive Catalogue of Plays and Dramatic Works (London: Samuel French, [1891?] onwards). Annually. Later called *Guide to Selecting Plays.*

Dissertation Abstracts, 1938 to the present (Ann Arbor, Michigan: University Microfilms).

Doctoral Dissertations Accepted by American Universities, ed. Arnold H. Trotier and Marian Harman (New York: H. W. Wilson, 1933–55). Continued as *Index to American Doctoral Dissertations*, 1955 to the present.

Dukore, Bernard F., ed. *A Bibliography of Theatre Arts Publications in English, 1963* (Washington: American Educational Theater Association, 1965). Contains both author and subject indexes.

Edyvean, Alfred R. *Religious Drama Project Play List* (New York: American Educational Theatre Association, n.d.). This mimeographed list of plays suitable for religious drama projects includes author, title, cast requirements, type of play, publisher and length of play.

Enser, A. G. S. *Filmed Books and Plays; A List of Books and Plays from Which Films Have Been Made, 1928–1967* (Elmsford, New York: London House and Maxwell, 1968; London: André Deutsch, 1971).

Essay and General Literature Index, 1900 to the present (New York: H. W. Wilson). Essays in books.

Etudes Irlandaises: Bulletin de Liaison des Specialistes Francophones d'Histoire, Civilisation et Litterature de l'Irlande (Lille-Cedex, France: CERIUL), 1972 to the present. Surveys activities of Irish studies in France and gives bibliographical information on publications and dissertations.

Goetsch, Paul and Heinz Kosok. 'Literatur zum modernen englischen Drama: Eine aüsgewählte Bibliographie,' *Das moderne englische Drama: Interpretationen*, ed. Horst Oppel, 2nd revised ed. (Berlin: Erich Schmidt, 1966), pp. 371–82. A selected secondary bibliography.

Green Room Book: Or Who's Who on the Stage—An Annual Bibliographical Record of the Dramatic, Musical and Variety World, 1906–9. Continued as *Who's Who in the Theatre: A Bibliographical Record of the Contemporary Stage*, 1912 to the present.

Guide to Reference Books, 1902 to the present (Chicago: American Library Association). Includes a section on 'English Drama.'

Harmon, Maurice. *Modern Irish Literature, 1800–1967; A Reader's Guide* (Dublin: Dolmen Press, 1967). Includes a section on 'Drama.'

Haskell, John D., Jr and Robert G. Shedd. 'Modern Drama: A Selective Bibliography of Works Published in English in 1966,' *Modern Drama,* X, no. 2 (September 1967), 202–15. Lists books and articles.

———. 'Modern Drama: A Selective Bibliography of Works Published in English in 1967,' *Modern Drama*, XI, no. 2 (September 1968), 195–213. Lists books and articles.

Hayman, Ronald. *One Hundred Years of Drama; A Selected List* (London: National Book League, 1972).

Holden, David F. *An Analytical Index to Modern Drama* (Toronto: Hakkert, 1972). Indexes articles in *Modern Drama*, vols I–XIII.

Hornby, Richard, comp. 'TDR Books and Theatre: A Bibliography,' *Tulane Drama Review*, IX, no. 4 (Summer 1965), 179–207. Listing of books published in the United States between 1 February 1964 and 31 January 1965.

———, comp. 'TDR Books and Theatre: A Bibliography,' *Tulane Drama Review*, X, no. 4 (Summer 1966), 239–64. Listing of books published in the United States between 1 February 1965 and 31 January 1966.

Howard, Diana, comp. *Directory of Theatre Research Resources in Greater London* (London: British Theatre Institute, 1974). A central catalogue of the collections of theatre material in London.

Hunter, Frederick J., ed. *A Guide to Theatre and Drama Collections at the University of Texas* (Austin, Texas: University of Texas Press, 1967). Catalogues some of the materials in the theatre and drama collections at the University of Texas.

———. *Drama Bibliography: A Short-Title Guide to Extended Reading in Dramatic Art for the English-Speaking Audience and Students in Theatre* (Boston: G. K. Hall, 1971). Selected lists arranged by subject matter.

Index to American Doctoral Dissertations, 1955 to the present (New York: H. W. Wilson). Continuation of

Doctoral Dissertations Accepted by American Universities, ed. Arnold H. Trotier and Marian Harman (New York: H. W. Wilson, 1933–55). Cumulative index by general subject matter and author.

An Index to Book Reviews in the Humanities, 1961 to the present (Williamston, Michigan: Phillip Thomson). Lists only reviews in English.

Index to Little Magazines, 1943 to the present (Denver, Colorado: Alan Swallow). An author-subject index of a selected list of American little magazines.

Index to Theses Accepted for Higher Degrees in the Universities of Great Britain and Ireland, 1950 to the present (London: ASLIB).

International Association for the Study of Anglo-Irish Literature. 'Bibliography Bulletin,' *Irish University Review; A Journal of Irish Studies* (Dublin), 1972 to the present. Lists books and articles on Anglo-Irish literature.

International Federation of Library Associations (International Section for Performing Arts Libraries and Museums). *Bibliotheque et musées des arts du spectacle dans le monde* (Paris: Editions du Centre National de la Recherche Scientifique, 1960); *Performing Arts Collection: An International Handbook* (New York: Theatre Arts, 1967). A fully revised and expanded edition of Rosamond Gilder's *Theatre Collections in Libraries and Museums*.

International Index to Periodicals, 1907 to the present (New York: H. W. Wilson), from vol. 19 (April 1965–March 1966) called *Social Sciences and Humanities Index*. Author and subject index to selected world periodicals.

'International Theatrediary,' *Theatrefacts; International Theatre Reference* (London), I, no. 1 (February 1974) to the present. Includes, in each issue, a survey of events and productions in 'Eire' and 'United Kingdom.'

Ireland, Norma Olin. *Index to Full Length Plays, 1944–1964* (Boston: F. W. Faxon, 1965). A selective coverage of full length plays published in English.

Johnson, Albert E. 'Doctoral Projects in Progress in Theatre Arts,' *Educational Theatre Journal*, VIII, no. 2 (May 1956) to the present. Listing furnishing the following information: the researcher's name, title, institution, supervisor, expected date of completion.

———. *Best Church Plays* (London: Pioneer Press, 1968). A bibliography of religious drama which features alphabetical listings, subject matter listings, and addresses of publishers, authors and agents. Pertinent information is given for each play.

Journal of Modern Literature (Temple University), 1970 to the present. Contains an Annual Review Number including a section on 'Criticism of Drama.'

Junge, Ewald. 'World Drama on Records,' *Theatre Research*, VI, no. 1 (1964), 16–49. A list of complete plays in their original language, published on long-playing records.

Kahn, A. M. C., ed. *Library Resources in the Greater London Area*, no. 4: *Theatre Collections; A Symposium* (London: Library Association, Reference and Special Libraries Section–South Eastern Group, 1953). A directory of libraries and institutions, grouped under the headings of national, public, special and private.

Keller, Dean H. *Index to Plays in Periodicals* (Metuchen, New Jersey: Scarecrow Press, 1971); *Supplement* (Metuchen, New Jersey: Scarecrow Press, 1973). Author–title index.

Knower, Franklin H. 'Graduate Theses in Theatre,' *Educational Theatre Journal,* III, no. 2 (May 1951), XV, no. 2 (May 1963). Lists dissertations submitted to American universities, classified under categories of subject matter.

Literature and Psychology, 1951 to the present. Includes an annual 'Bibliography' issued as a supplement to the fourth issue.

Literature, Music, Fine Arts: A Review of German-Language Research Contributions on Literature, Music, and Fine Arts, 1968. Biannual review of selected books and articles.

Litto, Fredric M. *American Dissertations on the Drama and the Theatre* (Kent, Ohio: Kent State University Press, 1969). Contains Author Index, Key Word-in-Context Index and Subject Index.

Logasa, Hannah, ed. *An Index to One-Act Plays: Fourth Supplement*, 1948–57 (Boston: F. W. Faxon, 1958); *An Index to One-Act Plays for Stage, Radio, and Television: Fifth Supplement 1956–1964* (Boston: F. W. Faxon, 1966). Contains titles of one-act plays written in English or translated into English from a foreign language. Author, number of characters, background and location of published play are given.

MLA Bibliography, 1919 to the present (New York: Modern Language Association of America). Basic reference lists of material in books and periodicals.

McNamee, Lawrence F. *Dissertations in English and American Literature: Theses Accepted by American, British and German Universities, 1865–1964* (New York and London: R. R. Bowker, 1968). *Supplement One* (New York and London: R. R. Bowker, 1969). *Supplement Two* (New York and London: R. R. Bowker, 1974).

Mellown, Elgin W. *A Descriptive Catalogue of the Bibliographies of 20th Century British Writers* (Troy, New York: Whitston Publishing Company, 1972). Lists primary and secondary bibliographies and checklists of British writers whose work appeared after 1890.

Mikhail, E. H. *A Bibliography of Modern Irish Drama 1899–1970*, with an introduction by William A. Armstrong (London: Macmillan; Seattle, Washington: University of Washington Press, 1972). Lists bibliographies, books, periodical articles and unpublished material devoted to modern Irish drama in general.

———. *Comedy and Tragedy: A Bibliography of Critical Studies* (Troy, New York: Whitston Publishing Company, 1972). Lists books and periodical articles.

———. *Dissertations on Anglo-Irish Drama: A Bibliography of Studies 1870–1970* (London: Macmillan; Totowa, New Jersey: Rowman and Littlefield, 1973). Indexed under general and individual dramatists.

New York Public Library. *Catalog of the Theatre and Drama Collections* (Boston: G. K. Hall, 1967). Entries are made under author, subject, title and other secondary headings.

New York Public Library. Berg Collection. *New In the Berg Collection, 1970–1972*, comp. Lola L. Szladits (New York: New York Public Library, 1973).

New York Public Library, Reference Department. *Theatre Subject Headings*, 2nd ed., enlarged (Boston: G. K. Hall, 1966). The subject headings are intended for use in the catalogue of the Theatre Collection of the Reference Department of the New York Public Library.

The New York Times Index, 1913 to the present. Arranged under subject headings.

Norton, Elizabeth Towne and Robert G. Shedd. 'Modern Drama: A Selective Bibliography of Works Published in English in 1959,' *Modern Drama,* III, no. 2 (September 1960), 143–61. Lists books and articles.

O'Mahony, Mathew. *Guide to Anglo-Irish Plays* (Dublin: Progress House, 1960). 'A survey of Anglo-Irish plays in suitable form for quick reference.' An up-to-date elaboration of the author's *Play Guide for Irish Amateurs*, published in 1947.

Ottemiller, John H. *Ottemiller's Index to Plays in Collections; An Author and Title Index to Plays Appearing in Collections Published between 1900 and Mid-1970*, by John M. Connor and Billie M. Connor (Metuchen, New Jersey: Scarecrow Press, 1971). The fifth edition of an index to plays appearing in 1280 published collections. Locates more than 9000 copies of 3500 different plays.

Palmer, Helen and Anne Jane Dyson. *European Drama Criticism* (Hamden, Connecticut: Shoe String Press, 1968); *Supplement I* (1970); *Supplement II* (1974). Lists studies of plays in books and periodicals.

Patterson, Charlotte A., comp. *Plays in Periodicals: An Index to English Language Scripts in Twentieth Century Journals* (Boston: G. K. Hall, 1970). '. . . gives access to over 4000 plays printed in ninety-seven English-language periodicals published from 1900 thru 1968.'

Play Index 1949–1952: An Index to 2616 Plays in 1138 Volumes, comp. Dorothy Herbert West and Dorothy Margaret Peake (New York: H. W. Wilson, 1953); *Play Index 1953–1960: An Index to 4592 Plays in 1735 Volumes*, ed. Estelle A. Fidell and Dorothy Margaret Peake (1963); *Play Index 1961–1967: An Index to 4793 Plays*, ed. Estelle A. Fidell (1968); *Play Index; An Index to 3848 Plays*, ed. Estelle A. Fidell (1973). Entries are indexed under author, title and subject.

Pownall, David E. *Articles on Twentieth Century Literature: An Annotated Bibliography 1954–1970* (Millwood, New York: Kraus-Thomson Organisation, 1973–). 'An expanded cumulation of "Current Bibliography" in the journal *Twentieth Century Literature*, Volume One to Volume Sixteen, 1955 to 1970.'

Reader's Guide to Books on Stagecraft and the Theatre, (London: Library Association, 1965). A select list of more than 400 mainly in-print books arranged under broad subject headings.

Readers' Guide to Periodical Literature, 1900 to the present (New York: H. W. Wilson). Author and subject index to selected world periodicals.

Research in Progress in English and Historical Studies in the Universities of the British Isles, 1971 to the present (London: St James Press).

Revue d'histoire du théâtre, 1948 to the present. Includes a 'Bibliographie,' indexed by subject matter.

Roberts, Peter. *Theatre in Britain* (London: Pitman, 1973). Includes a listing of major theatrical collections.

Royal Irish Academy, Committee for the Study of Anglo-Irish Language and Literature. *Handlist of Work in Progress,* (Dublin), 1969 to the present. Arranged under subject headings and individual writers.

Royal Irish Academy, Committee for the Study of Anglo-Irish Language and Literature. *Handlist of Theses Completed but Not Published* (Dublin), 1973 to the present. Lists dissertations on Irish writers.

Royal Irish Academy, Committee for the Study of Anglo-Irish Language and Literature. *Irish and Anglo-Irish*

Periodicals (Dublin: Royal Irish Academy, 1970). Lists and gives the locations in Ireland of all those periodicals which are likely to be of interest to scholars of Anglo-Irish literature.

Salem, James M. *A Guide to Critical Reviews, Part III: British and Continental Drama from Ibsen to Pinter*, (Metuchen, New Jersey: Scarecrow Press, 1968). Lists reviews of performances and criticism in periodicals.

———. *Drury's Guide to Best Plays* (Metuchen, New Jersey: Scarecrow Press, 1969). A second edition of the bibliography originally authored in 1953 by Francis K. W. Drury. Plays are listed by author with date of first performance or publication.

Samples, Gordon. *The Drama Scholars' Index to Plays and Filmscripts: A Guide to Plays and Filmscripts in Selected Anthologies, Series and Periodicals* (Metuchen, New Jersey: Scarecrow Press, 1974). Lists plays and filmscripts in their original languages, or in translations.

Santaniello, A. E. 'British Theatre: Nineteenth and Twentieth Century Drama,' *Theatre Books in Print; An Annotated Guide to the Literature of the Theatre, the Technical Arts of the Theatre, Motion Pictures, Television and Radio*, 2nd ed. (New York: Drama Book Shop, 1966), pp. 71–93.

Schoolcraft, Ralph Newman. *Performing Arts Books in Print: An Annotated Bibliography* (New York: Drama Book Specialists, 1973). Revised edition of *Theatre Books in Print*, originally published in 1963 and revised in 1966. Includes sections on 'Great Britain' and 'Ireland.'

Sharp, Harold S. and Marjorie Z. Sharp, comps. *Index to Characters in the Performing Arts; An Alphabetical Listing of 30,000 Characters. Part I: Non-Musical Plays*, 2 vols (Metuchen, New Jersey: Scarecrow Press, 1966). Identifies characters with the play in which they appear, indicates the author of the play, and shows the year in which the play was written, produced or published.

Shedd, Robert G. 'Modern Drama: A Selective Bibliography of Works Published in English in 1960 and 1961,' *Modern Drama,* V, no. 2 (September 1962), 223–44. Lists books and articles.

———. 'Modern Drama: A Selective Bibliography of Works Published in English in 1962,' *Modern Drama,* VI, no. 2 (September 1963), 204–17. Lists books and articles.

———. 'Modern Drama: A Selective Bibliography of Works Published in English in 1963–64,' *Modern Drama,* VIII, no. 2 (September 1965), 204–26. Lists books and articles.

———. 'Modern Drama: A Selective Bibliography of Works Published in English in 1965,' *Modern Drama,* IX, no. 2 (September 1966), 210–26. Lists books and articles.

Shipley, Joseph T. *Guide to Great Plays* (Washington, Public Affairs Press, 1956). Alphabetical listing of 660 masterpieces of world drama.

Simons, Eric N. 'The Library as a Tool of the Theatre,' *Aslib Proceedings* (London), I, no. 3 (November 1949), 271–8. On sources of information regarding the theatre.

Sobel, Bernard, ed. *The New Theatre Handbook and Digest of Plays* (New York: Crown Publishers, 1959). Includes bibliographies of works on plays and playwrights.

Social Sciences and Humanities Index, 1965 to the present. Continuation of *International Index to Periodicals*. Author and subject index to selected world periodicals.

Stratman, Carl J. 'Preparing a Bibliography of British Dramatic Periodicals, 1720–1960,' *Bulletin of the New*

York Public Library, LXVI (1962), 405–8. From the Introduction to the author's *A Bibliography of British Dramatical Periodicals 1720–1960.*

———, ed. *A Bibliography of British Dramatic Periodicals, 1720–1960* (New York: New York Public Library, 1962). A total of 670 titles are arranged chronologically with a note of locations in libraries, both in the USA and Great Britain, for complete files. Reprinted as *Britain's Theatrical Periodicals 1720–1967; A Bibliography* (New York: New York Public Library, 1972). A major revision of the original edition; indexes 1235 English periodicals; entries are descriptive.

Subject Index to Periodicals, 1915–1961 (London: Library Association). Continued as *British Humanities Index*, 1962 to the present. Subject and author index.

Temple, Ruth Z. and Martin Tucker, eds. *Twentieth Century British Literature; A Reference Guide and Bibliography* (New York: Frederick Ungar, 1968). Lists primary books and critical or bibliographical studies for each author.

Theatrefacts; International Theatre Reference (London), 1974 to the present. Incorporates and expands the reference material formerly included in *Theatre Quarterly.*

The Times Index (London), 1790 to the present. Subject index.

The Times Literary Supplement Index (London), 1902 to the present. Subject index.

Trewin, J. C., ed. *The Year's Work in the Theatre 1949–1950* (London: Longmans for the British Council, 1950). Survey.

———, ed. *The Year's Work in the Theatre 1950–1951* (London: Longmans for The British Council, 1951). Survey.

———. 'Books on the Theatre 1965–1969,' *British Book News* (September 1970), pp. 661–5; (October 1970), pp. 743–7. Annotated selected list.

Trussler, Simon. 'Current Bibliography,' *Theatre Quarterly* (London), 1971–3. Continued in *Theatrefacts; International Theatre Reference* (London), 1974 to present. A cumulative record of English-language books on theatre and related performing arts.

Tulane Drama Review, III (1959)–XI (1967). Includes 'Books and Theatre,' selected lists of books on drama and the theatre arranged by general subject.

Twentieth Century Literature, 1955 to the present. Contains regular quarterly annotated 'Current Bibliography' of critical literature in periodicals listed alphabetically, according to author of article.

Veinstein, André, ed. *Performing Arts Libraries and Museums of the World*, 2nd ed. (Paris: Editions du Centre National de la Recherche Scientifique, 1967). Originally published in 1960, this bilingual second edition, revised and enlarged by Cecile Giteau, is a census of all the known performing arts collections, libraries and museums throughout the world.

Vowles, Richard B. 'Psychology and Drama: A Selected Checklist,' *Wisconsin Studies in Contemporary Literature*, III, no. 1 (1962), 35–48. '. . . attempts to comprehend all relevant research and speculation since 1920.'

Welker, David, ed. '*Educational Theatre Journal*': *A Ten-Year Index: 1949–1958* (East Lansing, Michigan: Michigan State University, n.d.). Classified index of material published in the first ten volumes of the *Educational Theatre Journal*.

Willison, I. R., ed. 'Drama,' *The New Cambridge Bibliography of English Literature*, vol. 4: 1900–50 (Cambridge:

Cambridge University Press, 1972), cols 821–80. For most authors replaces *The Cambridge Bibliography of English Literature*.

Wilmeth, Don B. 'The Latest Decade of Theatre: Death or Deliverance?' *Choice,* VIII (February 1972), 1557–62. A selective bibliography including 'books which primarily deal with trends and directions of the past decade.'

Wilson, Sheila. *The Theatre of the 'Fifties*, with a foreword by Arnold Wesker, Special Subject List no. 40 (London: Library Association, 1963). Books and periodical articles on the theatre of this particular decade.

World Premieres (Paris: International Theatre Institute, 1949–64). Lists details of first productions of plays. Incorporated in *World Theatre*, 1965 to the present.

The Year's Work in English Studies, 1919 to the present (London: English Association). Annotated selective bibliography.

Reference Works

Includes encyclopaedias, dictionaries, glossaries, handbooks, guides and annuals

Anderson, Michael, *et al. Crowell's Handbook of Contemporary Drama* (New York: Thomas Y. Crowell, 1971; London: Pitman, 1972). An alphabetically arranged guide to written drama since World War II, with some critical appraisal of plays and playwrights as well as factual information.

Arts Council of Great Britain. *The Theatre Today: Annual Report* (London: Arts Council of Great Britain). Gives details of the state of the theatre each year, especially with regard to the grants given by the Council.

Barnet, Sylvan, Morton Berman and William Burto. *A Dictionary of Literary, Dramatic, and Cinematic Terms* (Boston: Little, Brown, 1971).

The Best Plays of 1950–52, ed. John Chapman, 2 vols (New York: Dodd, Mead, 1950–2). Includes an annual survey of 'The London Scene'.

The Best Plays of 1952–61, ed. Louis Kronenberger, 9 vols (New York: Dodd, Mead, 1952–61). Includes an annual survey of 'The London Scene.'

The Best Plays of 1961–64, ed. Henry Hewes, 3 vols (New York: Dodd, Mead, 1961–4). Includes an annual survey of 'The London Scene.'

The Best Plays of 1964–70, ed. Otis L. Guernsey, Jr, 6 vols (New York: Dodd, Mead, 1964–70). Includes an annual survey of 'The London Scene.'

Bowman, Walter Parke and Robert Hamilton Ball. *Theatre Language: A Dictionary of Terms in English of the Drama and Stage from Medieval to Modern Times* (New York: Theatre Arts, 1961). Technical and standard non-technical terms, jargon, cant and slang are defined and cross-referenced.

Britannica Book of the Year (London), 1938 to the present. Includes a survey of the preceding year's theatre work.

Buchanan-Brown, John, ed. *Cassell's Encyclopaedia of World Literature* (London: Cassell; West Caldwell, New Jersey: Morrow, 1973).

Burton, E. J. 'Contemporary Theatre 1940 Onwards,' *The Student's Guide to British Theatre and Drama* (London: Herbert Jenkins, 1963), pp. 162–76. Includes 'not only . . . the literary history of British drama but also the growth of British theatre.'

Cartmell, Van H., ed. 'British Plays,' *Plot Outlines of 100 Famous Plays* (Garden City, New York: Doubleday, 1962), pp. 83–241. Synopses of famous plays.

Dooley, Roger B. *Review Notes and Study Guide to Modern British and Irish Drama* (New York: Monarch Press, 1964). Introductory.

Drury, F. K. W. *Drury's Guide to Best Plays*, by James M. Salem, 2nd ed. (Metuchen, New Jersey: Scarecrow Press, 1969). Includes synopses of plays and guides for production.

Enciclopedia dello Spettacolo, 10 vols and appendix (Rome: Editrice le Maschere, 1954–68). By far the most comprehensive work on all aspects of the stage, cinema, radio and all related arts. Includes bibliographies and biographies and the coverage is universal.

Encyclopedia of Ireland (Dublin: Allen Figgis, 1968). Includes material on Irish drama.

Fay, W. G. *A Short Glossary of Theatrical Terms* (London and New York: Samuel French, [1930]). Reprinted from *Drama* (London).

Fleischmann, Wolfgang Bernard, ed. *Encyclopedia of World Literature in the 20th Century*, 3 vols (New York: Frederick Ungar, 1969).

Gassner, John and Edward Quinn, eds. *The Reader's Encyclopedia of World Drama* (New York: Thomas Y. Crowell, 1969). Gives information on plays and playwrights from all countries and has an appendix containing 'basic documents in dramatic theory.'

Granville, Wilfred. *A Dictionary of Theatrical Terms* (London: André Deutsch, 1952). American edition entitled *Theatre Dictionary* (New York: Oxford University Press, 1952). The compiler's aim was 'to record the technical, colloquial and slang terms . . . before many phrases used by 'old pros' died with their passing.'

Grigson, Geoffrey, ed. *The Concise Encyclopedia of Modern World Literature*, 2nd ed. (New York: Hawthorn Books, 1971). Contains mini-essays on individual writers.

Harmon, Maurice. *Modern Irish Literature 1800–1967; A Reader's Guide* (Dublin: Dolmen Press, 1967). 'The main intention was to open up the whole of modern Irish literature for study and exploration.'

Hartnoll, Phyllis, ed. *The Oxford Companion to the Theatre*, 3rd ed. (London: Oxford University Press, 1967).

Particular topics tend to be discussed under rather wide headings.

Harvey, Paul. *The Oxford Companion to English Literature,* 4th ed., revised by Dorothy Eagle (London and New York: Oxford University Press, 1967).

Hobson, Harold, ed. *International Theatre Annual* (London: Calder, 1956–60). An attempt was made to group contributions round a particular theme.

Holden, Michael. *The Stage Guide; Technical Information on British Theatres* (London: Carson and Comerford, 1971). A new and up-dated edition of the *Guide* published by the *Stage* periodical in 1912 and revised in 1946.

Holloway, John. 'The 20th Century: Drama,' *Encyclopaedia Britannica*, vol. 8 (London: Encyclopaedia Britannica, Inc., 1970), pp. 594–5.

International Theatre Annual, ed. Harold Hobson. (London: Calder, 1956–60). An attempt was made to group contributions round a particular theme.

International Theatre Institute. *World Premieres* (New York: UNESCO, 1949–64). Consists of a list, arranged by country, of first productions of new plays only, giving details of title, author and cast. From 1965 onwards it was incorporated in the International Theatre Institute's periodical *World Theatre.*

Johns, Eric, ed. *Theatre Review '73* (London and New York: W. H. Allen, 1973). '. . . the first of a series of annual publications.' Title later changed to *British Theatre Review 1974* (Eastbourne, East Sussex: Vance-Offord Publications, 1975). A record of all the major productions in London and the provinces.

Kienzle, Siegfried. *Modern World Theater: A Guide to Productions in Europe and the United States Since 1945*, trans. Alexander and Elizabeth Henderson (New York: Frederick Ungar, 1970). Some 580 plays are discussed.

Kunitz, Stanley J. and Howard Haycraft, eds. *Twentieth Century Authors, First Supplement* (New York: H. W. Wilson, 1955).

Leyson, Peter. *London Theatres: A Short History and Guide* (London: Apollo Publications, 1970). '. . . tries to give a handy guide to the main theatres, and a brief note of their history.'

Lounsbury, Warren C. *Theatre Backstage from A to Z* (Seattle and London: University of Washington Press, 1967). A dictionary of technical terms and methods.

McGraw–Hill Encyclopedia of World Drama (New York: McGraw–Hill, 1972), 4 vols.

Mander, Raymond and Joe Mitchenson. *The Theatres of London* (London: Hart-Davis, 1961; New York: Hill and Wang, 1962; paperback, 1964; new revised and enlarged ed., London: New English Library, 1975). A chronicle.

Matlaw, Myron. *Modern World Drama; An Encyclopedia* (New York: Dutton; London: Secker and Warburg, 1972).

May, Robin. *A Companion to the Theatre; The Anglo-American Stage from 1920* (London: Lutterworth Press, 1973). 'While dealing extensively with all the major theatrical genres, the author highlights certain plays and productions that are milestones in the story of the English-speaking theatre.'

Melchinger, Siegfried. *Drama Zwischen Shaw und Brecht: Ein Leitfaden durch das Zeitgenossische Schauspiel*, 2 Aufl.

(Bremen: Schunemann, 1957). A dictionary of both topics and dramatists.

———. *The Concise Encyclopedia of Modern Drama*, trans. George Wellwarth (New York: Horizon Press, 1964; London: Vision, 1966). The major part of the book is a biographical dictionary of some 800 playwrights. Analyses of plays, discussions of main trends, extensive glossary, important documents by leading dramatists, and a chronology of opening nights are provided.

Morley, Sheridan, ed. *Theatre 71* (London: Hutchinson, 1971). Collection of essays; 'the first of a series of annual volumes designed to give a continuing picture of the theatre as it evolves during the 1970's.'

———, ed. *Theatre 72* (London: Hutchinson, 1972).

———, ed. *Theatre 73* (London: Hutchinson, 1973).

Mueller, William R. 'English Literature: Modern Drama,' *Merit Students Encyclopedia* (New York: Crowell–Collier Educational Corporation, 1971), pp. 397–8.

New York Theatre Critics' Review, 1940 to the present (New York: Critics' Theatre Review). A periodical publication of the reviews of Broadway theatres reprinted from the seven major New York newspapers. Well indexed.

O'Mahony, Mathew. *Guide to Anglo-Irish Plays* (Dublin: Progress House, 1960). 'A survey of Anglo-Irish plays in suitable form for quick reference.' An up-to-date elaboration of the author's *Play Guide for Irish Amateurs*, published in 1947.

Page, Malcolm. 'Experimental Theatre in London,' *Kansas Quarterly*, III, no. 2 (1971), 118–26. A guide to the 'Off-West-End.'

Pride, Leo B., ed. *International Theatre Directory: A World Directory of the Theatre and Performing Arts* (New York: Simon and Schuster, 1973). Within each of the countries, the theatres are presented under cities and towns.

Rae, Kenneth and Richard Southern, eds. *International Vocabulary of Technical Theatre Terms in Eight Languages* (Brussels: Elsevier; New York: Reinhart, 1959; Theatre Arts, 1960). Compiled for the International Theatre Institute. Theatre terms used are American, Dutch, English, French, German, Italian, Spanish and Swedish.

Roberts, Peter. *Theatre in Britain; A Playgoer's Guide* (London: Pitman, 1973). Provides 'guidelines–for the visitor to Britain in particular.'

Runes, Dagobert D. and Harry G. Schrikel, eds. *Encyclopedia of the Arts* (New York: Philosophical Library, 1946; Owen, 1964). '. . . a comprehensive survey of all the arts of all times and all places.'

Schorer, Mark. 'The Late 1950's and Beyond,' *The Encyclopedia Americana,* international ed., vol. 10 (New York: Americana Corporation, 1972), p. 453.

Shank, Theodore J., ed. *A Digest of 500 plays: Plot Outlines and Production Notes* (New York: Collier Books; London: Collier–Macmillan, 1966).

Sharp, Harold S. and Marjorie Z. Sharp, comps. *Index to Characters in the Performing Arts; An Alphabetical Listing of 30,000 Characters. Part I: Non-Musical Plays*, 2 vols (Metuchen, New Jersey: Scarecrow Press, 1966). Identifies characters with the play in which they appear, tells something about the character, indicates the author of the play, and shows the year in which the play was written, produced or published.

Shipley, Joseph T. *Guide to Great Plays* (Washington: Public Affairs Press, 1956). Gives a digest of each play in addition to information on famous productions, casts and reviews.

Sobel, Bernard, ed. *The New Theatre Handbook and Digest of Plays* (New York: Crown Publishers, 1959). A revision of the 1940 edition, this volume contains synopses of plays, glossaries of theatre terms, biographies, information on productions and bibliographies.

Spencer, Terence John Bew. 'The 20th Century: Drama,' *Chambers's Encyclopaedia*, new revised ed., vol. V (Oxford: Pergamon Press, 1966), p. 317.

Spinchorn, Evert, ed. *20th-Century Plays in Synopsis* (New York: Thomas Y. Crowell, 1965). Act-by-act synopses of 133 representative modern plays and biographical information on playwrights.

Stacey, R. *Plays: A Classified Guide to Play Selection 1957–1965* (Bromley, Kent: Stacey Publications, 1959–66). Classified according to type, with details of cast, publisher, price, etc.

The Stage and Television Today Year Book, 1908 to the present (London: Carson and Comerford). Gives overall picture of the previous year in a few short articles and lists names of managements, professional organisations, etc.

Taylor, John Russell. *The Penguin Dictionary of the Theatre* (Harmondsworth, Middlesex: Penguin Books, 1966; New York: Barnes and Noble, 1967). Despite its title, it is really a miniature encyclopaedia.

The Thames and Hudson Encyclopaedia of the Arts (London: Thames and Hudson, 1966). Biographies, definitions of technical terms and brief accounts of movements; no general articles.

Theatre World Annual, 1949–63 (London: Barrie and Rockliff); 1964– (London: Iliffe). Indexes the plays and players featured in its largely pictorial survey of the major London productions.

Trewin, J. C., ed. *The Year's Work in the Theatre, 1948–1951*, 3 vols (London: Longmans for the British Council, 1949–51). Review of the year in the theatre. Discontinued.

Vinson, James, ed. *Contemporary Dramatists.* With a preface by Ruby Cohn (London: St James Press; New York: St Martin's Press, 1973). An extensive reference guide to the most important living playwrights in the English language.

Ward, A. C. *Longman Companion to Twentieth Century Literature*, 2nd ed. (London: Longman, 1975). '. . . a compact handbook.'

Who's Who in the Theatre: A Biographical Record of the Contemporary Stage, 1912 to the present (London: Pitman). Includes, as well as biographies of all well-known living personalities of the theatre, much other information, including genealogical tables, obituaries, dates of notable productions, etc.

Young, Derek, ed. *Stagecast: Irish Stage and Screen Directory* (Dublin: Stagecast Publications). Annually from 1962.

Books

Allsop, Kenneth. *The Angry Decade; A Survey of the Cultural Revolt of the Nineteen-Fifties* (London: Peter Owen; New York: British Book Centre, 1958). On the young dramatists who have come up through the Royal Court, the Arts Theatre and the Theatre Workshop.

Ansorge, Peter. 'Notes from the Underground,' *Theatre 74*, ed. Sheridan Morley (London: Hutchinson, 1974), pp. 107–17. A report on the alternative theatre.

———. *Disrupting the Spectacle; Five Years of Experimental and Fringe Theatre in Britain* (London and New York: Pitman, 1975). 'The author pieces together the fringe's fragmented history.'

Armstrong, William A., ed. *Experimental Drama* (London: G. Bell, 1963; New York: Dufour, 1965). Contributions by William A. Armstrong, Geoffrey Bullough, Martin Esslin, Eric Gillett, Laurence Kitchin, J. C. Trewin, Dennis Welland and Katharine J. Worth.

———. 'The Irish Dramatic Movement,' *Classic Irish Drama* (Harmondsworth, Middlesex: Penguin, 1964), pp. 7–15. Survey.

Arts Council of Great Britain. *The Theatre Today: Annual Report* (London: Arts Council of Great Britain). Gives details of the state of the theatre each year.

Baleanu, Andrei. *Teatrul furiei si al violentei. Privire asupra dramaturgiei americane si engleze (1956–1966).* [The theatre of rage and violence. An examination of the American and English drama.] (Bucharest: Editura pentru literatura universala, 1967.)

Barnet, Sylvan, Morton Berman and William Burto, eds. 'The English Theatre Since 1660: An Introduction,' *The Genius of the Later English Theater* (New York: New American Library, 1962), pp. 7–20. Introductory survey.

Baxter, Beverley. *First Nights and Footlights* (London: Hutchinson, 1955). Criticisms from the *Evening Standard*, 1948–54.

Baxter, Kathleen M. *Speak What We Feel: A Christian Looks at the Contemporary Theatre* (London: SCM Press, 1964). American edition entitled *Contemporary Theatre and the Christian Faith* (Nashville, Tennessee: Abingdon Press, 1964). 'The aim of this short book is to observe the points at which the "new" theatre can illuminate some of the problems which Christians face in understanding and communicating their faith.'

Beckerman, Bernard. *Dynamics of Drama; The Theory and Method of Analysis* (New York: Alfred A. Knopf, 1970). Makes some illustrations from modern British plays.

Bell, Sam H. 'Theatre,' *Causeway: The Arts in Ulster*, ed. Michael Longley (Belfast: Arts Council of Northern Ireland, 1971), pp. 83–94. Survey.

———. *The Theatre in Ulster: A Survey of the Dramatic Movement in Ulster from 1902 to the Present Day* (Totowa, New Jersey: Rowman and Littlefield; Dublin: Gill and Macmillan, 1972).

Bermel, Albert. *Contradictory Characters; An Interpretation of the Modern Theatre* (New York: E. P. Dutton; Toronto: Clarke, Irwin, 1973). Includes essays on Samuel Beckett and Harold Pinter.

Billington, Michael. 'Our Theatres in the Sixties,' *Theatre 71*, ed. Sheridan Morley (London: Hutchinson, 1971), pp. 208–33. The deputy drama critic of *The Times* looks back over the decade in which he started visiting the theatre professionally.

———. 'The National Theatre: Olivier's Final Year,' *Theatre 74*, ed. Sheridan Morley (London: Hutchinson, 1974), pp. 49–59. The drama critic of the *Guardian* reviews the Old and Young Vic companies.

Bloomfield, Roderick, ed. *Heard in the Wings* (London: Stanley Paul, 1971). Anecdotes by various hands.

Blunt, Jerry. *Stage Dialects* (San Francisco, California: Chandler Publishing Company, 1967), pp. 51–90. Includes chapters on Standard English, Cockney, Irish, Scots.

Blythe, Ernest. *The Abbey Theater* (Dublin: National Theatre Society, [1965]). A brochure.

Bradbrook, M. C. 'The English Revival,' *English Dramatic Form: A History of Its Development* (London: Chatto and Windus; New York: Barnes and Noble, 1965), pp. 186–91.

Brahms, Caryl. *The Rest of the Evening's My Own* (London: W. H. Allen, 1964). Collected reviews.

Brandt, G. W. 'Realism and Parables: From Brecht to Arden,' *Contemporary Theatre*, ed. John Russell Brown and Bernard Harris, Stratford-upon-Avon Studies, 4 (London:

Edward Arnold, 1961; New York: St Martin's Press, 1962), pp. 33–55. Survey.

Bredsdorff, Thomas. 'Det ny engelske teater og dets forfattere,' *Fremmede digtere i det 20. århundrede*, vol. III, ed. Sven M. Kristensen (Copenhagen: G. E. C. Grad, 1968), pp. 569–86. Deals with John Osborne, Arnold Wesker and Harold Pinter.

Brockett, Oscar G. 'English Theatre and Drama Since 1945,' *History of the Theatre* (Boston: Allyn and Bacon, 1968), pp. 672–80. Survey.

——— and Robert R. Findlay. *Century of Innovation: A History of European and American Theatre and Drama Since 1870* (Englewood Cliffs, New Jersey: Prentice–Hall, 1973). A new historical survey of major trends in Western theatre and drama.

Brook, Peter. *The Empty Space* (London: MacGibbon and Kee, 1968; Harmondsworth, Middlesex: Penguin Books, 1972). 'One of the world's most famous directors gives us the distillation of his knowledge and experience of the theatre.'

Brown, Ivor. *Theatre, 1954–5* (London: Max Reinhardt, 1955). Reviews of the season's plays. Lists central London and principal repertory productions.

———. *Theatre, 1955–6* (London: Max Reinhardt, 1956). Reviews of the season's plays. Lists central London and principal repertory productions.

Brown, John Russell, ed. *Modern British Dramatists; A Collection of Critical Essays* (Englewood Cliffs, New Jersey: Prentice–Hall, 1968). Essays on general aspects and on individual playwrights: John Osborne, Harold Pinter, Arnold Wesker and John Arden.

———. *Theatre Language; A Study of Auden, Osborne, Pinter and Wesker* (London: Allen Lane The Penguin Press; New York: Taplinger, 1972).

——— and Bernard Harris, eds. *Contemporary Theatre*, Stratford-upon-Avon studies, no. 4 (London: Edward Arnold, 1961; New York: St Martin's Press, 1962). See articles under individual contributors: Clifford Leech, G. W. Brandt, A. R. Jones, Allardyce Nicoll, Kenneth Muir, R. D. Smith, John Jordan and J. L. Styan.

Browne, E. Martin, ed. *New English Dramatists*, nos 1–3 (Harmondsworth, Middlesex: Penguin, 1959). Contains introductions by the editor on the dramatists concerned.

———, ed. 'Introduction,' *Three Irish Plays* (Harmondsworth, Middlesex: Penguin Books, 1959). Anthology.

Brustein, Robert. *The Theatre of Revolt: An Approach to the Modern Drama* (Boston: Atlantic–Little, Brown, 1964; London: Methuen, 1965). Suggests an approach to the modern drama as a whole.

———. *Seasons of Discontent; Dramatic Opinions 1959–1965* (New York: Simon and Schuster, 1965; London: Jonathan Cape, 1966). Articles and reviews from various periodicals, mainly the *New Republic*.

———. 'The English Stage,' *Modern British Dramatists; A Collection of Critical Essays*, ed. John Russell Brown (Englewood Cliffs, New Jersey: Prentice–Hall, 1968), pp. 164–70. Reprinted from *New Statesman* (London), LXX (6 August 1965), 193–4.

———. *The Third Theatre* (London: Jonathan Cape, 1970). Articles and reviews from various periodicals.

Bryden, Bill. 'Bricks on Our Shoulders: The Theatre in Scotland,' *Theatre 74*, ed. Sheridan Morley (London: Hutchinson, 1974), pp. 126–31. The theatre in Scotland,

and the need for a Scottish theatre, as seen by the associate director of Edinburgh's Royal Lyceum.

Bryden, Ronald. *The Unfinished Hero and Other Essays* (London: Faber and Faber, 1969). Includes reviews of productions staged during the period when the author was the *New Statesman's* drama critic.

———. 'The National's Health,' *Theatre 71*, ed. Sheridan Morley (London: Hutchinson, 1971), pp. 33–47. An astringent look at a year in the life of the National Theatre by the retiring drama critic of the *Observer*.

Burns, Elizabeth. *Theatricality; A Study of Convention in the Theatre and in Social Life* (London: Longman, 1972). Makes references to some modern British dramatists.

Burton, Hal, ed. *Acting in the Sixties* (London: BBC Publications, 1970).

Caboche, Lucien. 'L'Influence de la guerre sur les tendances actuelles,' *Le Theatre en Grande-Bretagne pendant la seconde guerre mondiale* (Paris: Marcel Didier, 1969), pp. 261–313. Survey.

Calderwood, James L. and Harold E. Toliver, eds. *Perspectives on Drama* (New York and London: Oxford University Press, 1968). Collection of essays on dramatic theory.

Chapman, John, ed. 'The London Scene,' *The Best Plays of 1950–52*, 2 vols (New York: Dodd, Mead, 1950–2). An annual survey.

Chiari, J. 'Drama in England,' *Landmarks of Contemporary Drama* (London: Herbert Jenkins, 1965; New York: Hillary House, 1966; New York: Gordian Press, 1971), pp. 107–34. Survey.

Cleaver, James. 'The English Theatre of the Twentieth Century,' *Theatre Through the Ages* (New York: Hart Publishing Company, 1967), pp. 295–355. Survey.

Clurman, Harold. 'The Theatre of England,' *Lies Like Truth* (New York: Macmillan, 1958), pp. 161–94. Reports on productions and short essays on some leading players.

———. *The Naked Image; Observations on the Modern Theatre* (New York: Macmillan; London: Collier–Macmillan, 1966). Reports on productions.

———. *The Divine Pastime; Theatre Essays* (New York: Macmillan; London: Collier–Macmillan, 1974). Reprinted material.

Cohn, Ruby. 'English Language Drama,' *Currents in Contemporary Drama* (Bloomington, Indiana, and London: Indiana University Press, 1969), pp. 3–17. Survey.

Corrigan, Robert W., ed. *Theatre in the Twentieth Century* (New York: Grove Press, 1963). Anthology of criticism from *Tulane Drama Review*.

———. 'Anger and After: A Decade of the British Theatre,' *The Theatre in Search of a Fix* (New York: Delacorte Press, 1973), pp. 301–24. Discusses Robert Bolt, Ann Jellicoe, John Osborne, Harold Pinter and John Arden.

Corsani, Mary. *Il Nuovo Teotro Inglese* (Milan: U. Mursia, 1970). Deals with most contemporary British dramatists.

Cowell, Raymond. *Twelve Modern Dramatists* (Oxford: Pergamon Press, 1967). Includes Arnold Wesker, Samuel Beckett and Harold Pinter.

Dace, Letitia. *Modern Theatre and Drama* (New York: Richards Rosen Press, 1973), pp. 110–14. Survey.

Dane, Clemence. *Approaches to Drama*, English Association Presidential Address, 1961 (London: Oxford University Press, 1961). Pamphlet dealing with the new 'moods in which people go to a play.'

Davison, P. H. 'Contemporary Drama and Popular Dramatic Forms,' *Aspects of Drama and the Theatre*, by Richard N. Coe *et al.*, with a preface by A. K. Stout (Sydney: Sydney University Press; London: Methuen, 1965), pp. 143–97. Discusses with many examples the influence on English drama of music hall, pantomime, radio and television.

Day, Martin S. 'English Drama from Shaw to the Present,' *History of English Literature 1837 to the Present* (Garden City, New York: Doubleday, 1964), pp. 273–98.

De Jongh, Nicholas. 'Notes from the Underground,' *Theatre 73*, ed. Sheridan Morley (London: Hutchinson, 1973), pp. 46–58. The arts reporter of the *Guardian* looks back at the past twelve months on the 'fringe.'

Dennis, Nigel. *Dramatic Essays* (London: Weidenfeld and Nicolson, 1962). Includes references to some modern British dramatists.

Dietrich, Margaret. *Das Moderne Drama: Stromungen–Gestalten–Motive* (Stuttgart: Alfred Kroner, 1961). Includes studies of John Osborne, Harold Pinter and Samuel Beckett.

Dobbs, Brian. *Drury Lane: Three Centuries of the Theatre Royal, 1663–1971* (London: Cassell, 1972). Survey.

Dooley, Roger B. *Modern British and Irish Drama*, Monarch Review Notes & Study Guide Series, no. 624 (New York: Thor Publications, 1964). Introductory.

Drescher, Horst W. 'Angry Young Men' and 'Reformers and Absurdists,' *World Literature Since 1945*, ed. Ivar Ivask and Gero von Wilpert (New York: Frederick Ungar, 1973), pp. 90–103. Survey essays.

Driver, Tom F. *Romantic Quest and Modern Query; A History of the Modern Theater* (New York: Dell Publishing Company, 1970). References to some modern British plays.

Duprey, Richard A. *Just Off the Aisle: The Ramblings of a Catholic Critic* (Westminster, Maryland: Newman Press, 1962). Includes studies of Paul Vincent Carroll, Brendan Behan and Robert Bolt.

Edwards, Hilton. 'The Irish Theatre,' *A History of the Theatre*, by George Freedley and John A. Reeves, 3rd revised ed. (New York: Crown Publishers, 1968), pp. 735–48. Survey.

Elsom, John. *Erotic Theatre* (London: Secker and Warburg, 1973). Contrasts the treatment of sex in the theatre during two particular historical periods–from 1890 to 1910 and from 1950 to the present.

Elvin, B. 'Introduction,' *Teatrul englez contemporan* [Contemporary English Drama] (Bucharest: Editura pentru literatura universala, 1968), pp. 5–28. Survey.

Esslin, Martin. *The Theatre of the Absurd* (Garden City, New York: Doubleday, 1961; London: Eyre and Spottiswoode, 1962; revised ed., Garden City, New York: Doubleday, 1969; revised updated ed., Woodstock, New York: Over look Press, 1973). Includes essays on Samuel Beckett, Harold Pinter and N. F. Simpson.

———. 'Godot and His Children: The Theatre of Samuel Beckett and Harold Pinter,' *Experimental Drama*, ed. William A. Armstrong (London: G. Bell, 1963; New York: Dufour, 1965), pp. 128–46.

———. *Reflections; Essays on Modern Theatre* (Garden City, New York: Doubleday, 1969). British edition entitled *Brief Chronicles; Essays on Modern Theatre* (London: Temple Smith, 1970). 'Always he sees the theatre as a reflection of the society that produced it.'

Evans, Sir Ifor. 'Contemporary Drama,' *A Short History of English Drama* (Boston: Houghton Mifflin, 1965), pp. 188–208. Survey.

Fallon, Gabriel, ed. *Abbey Theatre 1904–1966* (Dublin: National Theatre Society, 1966). Brochure to mark the opening of the new Abbey Theatre in 1966.

Fechter, Paul. *Das Europaische Drama: Geist und Kultur im Spiegel des Theaters*., vol. III (Mannheim: Bibliographisches Institut Ag., 1958). Includes studies of Graham Greene, Peter Ustinov, Dylan Thomas, John Osborne, Samuel Beckett, Enid Bagnold, John Hall and John van Druten.

Findlater, Richard. *The Future of the Theatre* (London: Fabian Society, 1959). Pamphlet examining the state of the English theatre and suggesting some measures which must be taken.

———. *Banned! A Review of Theatrical Censorship in Britain* (London: MacGibbon and Kee, 1967).

Forbes-Robertson, Diana and Andre van Gyseghem. 'England (1955–1965),' *A History of the Theatre*, by George Freedley and John A. Reeves, 3rd revised ed. (New York: Crown Publishers, 1968), pp. 728–34. Survey.

Fraser, G. S. 'The Drama: The Wind of Change in the 1950's,' *The Modern Writer and His World*, revised ed. (London: André Deutsch, 1964), pp. 227–44. Survey.

Freedman, Morris, ed. *Essays in the Modern Drama* (Boston: D. C. Heath, 1964). Includes essays by various hands on Samuel Beckett, John Osborne and Harold Pinter.

———. 'From Anger to Absurdity,' *The Moral Impulse: Modern Drama from Ibsen to the Present* (Carbondale and Edwardsville, Illinois: Southern Illinois University Press; London and Amsterdam: Feffer and Simon, 1967), pp. 115–27. Includes references to Samuel Beckett and Harold Pinter.

Fricker, Robert. *Das moderne englische Drama* (Gottingen: Vandenhoeck and Ruprecht, 1964). Includes studies of Samuel Beckett, Brendan Behan, Robert Bolt, Shelagh Delaney, John Osborne, Harold Pinter, Peter Shaffer, N. F. Simpson, Peter Ustinov, Arnold Wesker and John Whiting.

Frow, Gerald, ed. *The Mermaid Theatre: The First Ten Years* (London: Mermaid Theatre, 1969). Review of the Theatre 1959–69 published to mark its tenth anniversary.

Gaiety Theatre, Dublin. 1871–1971: One Hundred Years of Gaiety (Dublin: Gaiety Theatre, 1971).

Gascoigne, Bamber, 'The New Playwrights—Great Britain: Osborne, Wesker, Behan, Delaney, Whiting, Bolt, Arden, Pinter,' *Twentieth-Century Drama* (London: Hutchinson, 1962; New York: Barnes and Noble, 1968), pp. 196–208. Survey.

Gassner, John. *Dramatic Soundings* (New York: Crown Publishers, 1968). Essays and reviews including some on contemporary British dramatists.

Gielgud, Val. *British Radio Drama, 1922–1956*, with a foreword by Sir William Haley (London and Toronto: George G. Harrap, 1957). A study by the Head of BBC drama for twenty-nine years.

Gillett, Eric. 'Regional Realism: Shelagh Delaney, Alun Owen, Keith Waterhouse, and Willis Hall,' *Experimental Drama*, ed. William A. Armstrong (London: G. Bell, 1963; New York: Dufour, 1965), pp. 186–203.

Gilliatt, Penelope. *Unholy Fools: Wits, Comics, Disturbers of the Peace–Film and Theatre* (London: Secker and Warburg, 1973). A 'compendium of her film and theater writing, drawn from more than a decade's reviewing and reportage on both sides of the Atlantic.'

Goetsch, Paul. 'Das Gesellschaftsdrama seit 1940,' *Das Englische Drama*, ed. Josefa Nünning (Darmstadt: Wissenschaftliche Buchgesellschaft, 1973), pp. 427–507. Survey.

———, ed. *English Dramatic Theories: 20th Century*, English Texts 13, gen. ed. Theo Stemmler (Tübingen: Max Niemeyer, 1972), pp. 99–123. Includes critical writings by John Whiting, John Osborne, Arnold Wesker, John Arden and Harold Pinter.

Gottfried, Martin. *Opening Nights; Theater Criticism of the Sixties* (New York: G. P. Putnam's, 1969). Reprinted material including reviews of some contemporary British plays.

Gozenpud, A. *Puti i pereput'ya. Angliiskaya i frantsuzskaya dramaturgiya xx v* [Roads and Cross-Roads. English and French 20th Century Drama] (Leningrad: Iskusstvo, 1967). Includes studies of Samuel Beckett, Brendan Behan, Shelagh Delaney, John Osborne, Harold Pinter and N. F. Simpson.

Guernsey, Otis L., Jr. 'The London Scene,' *The Best Plays of 1964–70*, 6 vols (New York: Dodd, Mead, 1964–70). An annual survey.

Guerrero Zamora, Juan. 'Inglaterra, 1956–1965,' *Historia del teatro contemporaneo*, vol. 4 (Barcelona: Juan Flors, 1967), pp. 1–42. Includes discussions of John Osborne, Shelagh Delaney, Arnold Wesker, John Arden and Brendan Behan.

Hahnloser-Ingold, Margrit. *Das englische Theater und Bert Brecht. Die Dramen von W. H. Auden, John Osborne, John Arden in ihrer Beziehung zum epischem Theater von Bert Brecht und den gemeinsamen elisabethanischen Quellen*, Swiss Studies in English, 61 (Bern: A. Francke, 1970). The influence of Brecht's epic theatre on the plays of W. H. Auden, John Osborne and John Arden.

Hammerschmidt, Hildegard. *Das historische Drama in England (1956–1971): Erscheinungsformen und Entwicklungstenzen* (Wiesbaden: Humanitas, 1972). Examines historical plays by Robert Bolt, Terence Rattigan, Christopher Fry, John Osborne, John Whiting, James Saunders, David Pinner and John Arden.

Hartley, Anthony. 'The London Stage: Drugs No Answer,' *Theatre in Review,* ed. Frederick Lumley (Edinburgh: Richard Paterson, 1956), pp. 1–15. Reflections on the present state.

Hartnoll, Phyllis. 'The Modern Theatre,' *A Concise History of the Theatre* (London: Thames and Hudson, 1968; paperback ed., 1971), pp. 240–67. '. . . a history of the theatre in the widest sense.'

Haskell, Stephen. 'Situation du théâtre en Angleterre,' *Situation de la Littérature Anglaise d'Aprés-Guerre*, ed. Ronald Hayman (Paris: Lettres Modernes, 1955), pp. 129–36. Survey since 1945.

Hatlen, Theodore W. *Orientation to the Theater*, 2nd ed. (New York: Appleton–Century–Crofts, 1972). A Study of various aspects of the drama making some references to modern British plays.

Hayman, Ronald. 'Le Théâtre commercial,' *Situation de la Littérature d'Après-Guerre* (Paris: Lettres Modernes, 1955), pp. 154–60. Survey since 1945.

———. *The Set-Up; An Anatomy of the English Theatre Today* (London: Eyre Methuen, 1973). Deals with various aspects of the contemporary British theatre.

———. *Playback* (London: Davis–Poynter, 1973). Interviews.

———. *Playback 2* (London: Davis–Poynter, 1973). Interviews.

Heilman, Robert B. *Tragedy and Melodrama; Versions of Experience* (Seattle and London: University of Washington Press, 1968). Includes some illustrations from modern British plays.

———. *The Iceman, the Arsonist, and the Troubled Agent; Tragedy and Melodrama on the Modern Stage* (Seattle: University of Washington Press; London: George Allen and Unwin, 1973). Examination of tragic and melodramatic styles begun in *Tragedy and Melodrama*.

Hewes, Henry, ed. 'The London Scene,' *The Best Plays of 1961–64*, 3 Vols (New York: Dodd, Mead, 1961–4). An annual survey.

Hewitt, Barnard. *History of the Theatre from 1800 to the Present* (New York: Random House, 1970). Survey.

Hickey, Des and Gus Smith. *A Paler Shade of Green* (London: Leslie Frewin, 1972). American edition entitled *Flight from the Celtic Twilight* (Indianapolis, Indiana:

Bobbs–Merrill, 1973). '. . . mirrors the significant events in theatrical and cinematic history which have been influenced by the Irish since the turn of the century,'

Hinchcliffe, Arnold P. *The Absurd, The Critical Idiom*, 5 (London: Methuen, 1969). Introductory booklet.

———. 'Drama,' *The Twentieth-Century Mind: History, Ideas, and Literature in Britain, vol. III–1945–1965*, ed. C. B. Cox and A. E. Dyson (London and New York: Oxford University Press, 1972), pp. 414–39. Survey.

———. *British Theatre, 1950–1970* (Oxford: Basil Blackwell; Totowa, New Jersey: Rowman and Littlefield, 1974). Survey

Hobson, Harold. *The Theatre Now* (London and New York: Longmans, 1953). Reviews reprinted from the *Sunday Times*, 1949–52.

Hogan, Robert. *After the Irish Renaissance; A Critical History of the Irish Drama Since 'The Plough and the Stars'* (Minneapolis, Minnesota: University of Minnesota Press, 1967; London: Macmillan, 1968). '. . . an informal critical account.'

———. 'Where Have All the Shamrocks Gone?' *Aspects of the Irish Theatre*, ed. Patrick Rafroidi, Raymonde Popot and William Parker (Lille: PUL; Paris: Editions Universitaires, 1972), pp. 261–71. Argues that the Irishness of Irish drama will become extinct.

Hortmann, Wilhelm. *Englische Literatur im 20. Jahrhundert* (Bern: A. Francke, 1965). Deals with John Osborne, John Arden, Arnold Wesker, Brendan Behan, Shelagh Delany, Harold Pinter, N. F. Simpson and John Whiting.

Houghton, Norris. *The Exploding Stage; An Introduction to Twentieth Century Drama* (New York: Weybright and

Talley, 1971; Delta Book, 1973). Includes illustrations from some modern British plays.

Hunt, James, ed. *Focus on Film and Theatre* (Englewood Cliffs, New Jersey: Prentice–Hall, 1974). Anthology making a few references to modern British plays.

Hunter, G. K. 'English Drama 1900–1960,' *History of Literature in the English Language. Vol. 7: The Twentieth Century*, ed. Bernard Bergonzi (London: Sphere Books, 1970), pp. 310–35. Survey.

Hunter, N. C. *Modern Trends in the Theatre.* The W. D. Thomas Memorial Lecture (Swansea, Wales: University College, 1969). Brief survey.

Irving, Wardle. 'Let Them Eat Bread,' *Theatre 72*, ed. Sheridan Morley (London: Hutchinson, 1972), pp. 50–62. A year in the life of the National Theatre, reviewed by the drama critic of *The Times*.

Jellicoe, Ann. *Some Unconscious Influences in the Theatre*, the Judith Wilson Lecture 1967 (Cambridge: Cambridge University Press, 1967). Pamphlet.

Johns, Eric, ed. *Theatre Review '73* (London and New York: W. H. Allen, 1973). '. . . the first of a series of annual publications.'

Jordan, John. 'The Irish Theatre–Retrospect and Premonition,' *Contemporary Theatre*, ed. John Russell Brown and Bernard Harris. Stratford-upon-Avon Studies, 4 (London: Edward Arnold, 1961; New York: St Martin's Press, 1962), pp. 165–83. Survey.

Kennedy, Andrew. *Six Dramatists in Search of a Language: Studies in Dramatic Language* (Cambridge: Cambridge University Press, 1974). Includes discussions of Samuel Beckett, Harold Pinter, John Osborne and John Arden.

Kernodle, George R. *Invitation to the Theatre* (New York: Harcourt, Brace and World, 1967). Considers all major forms of theatre, with several illustrations from modern British plays.

Kerr, Walter. *The Theater in Spite of Itself* (New York: Simon and Schuster, 1963). Includes reviews of plays by Brendan Behan, Harold Pinter, Shelagh Delaney, John Osborne and Robert Bolt.

———. *Tragedy and Comedy* (New York: Simon and Schuster, 1967; London: Bodley Head, 1968). Includes some illustrations from modern British plays.

———. *Thirty Plays Hath November; Pain and Pleasure in the Contemporary Theater* (New York: Simon and Schuster, 1969). Reprinted essays making some references to modern British plays.

Kershaw, John. *The Present Stage: New Directions in the Theatre Today*, Fontana Books (London: Collins, 1966). Includes chapters on John Osborne, Arnold Wesker, Harold Pinter and Samuel Beckett.

Khan, Naseem. 'Notes from the Underground,' *Theatre 72*, ed. Sheridan Morley (London: Hutchinson, 1972), pp. 28–36. The co-editor of *Time Out's* Theatre section looks at the past twelve months on the 'fringe.'

Killinger, John. *World in Collapse; The Vision of Absurd Drama* (New York: Dell, 1971). Survey and evaluation of the Theatre of the Absurd.

Kingston, Jeremy. 'Year of the Flash: the West End,' *Theatre 73*, ed. Sheridan Morley (London: Hutchinson, 1973), pp. 37–45. The playwright and drama critic of *Punch* surveys the year in the commercial theatre.

Kitchen, Laurence. *Mid-Century Drama* (London: Faber and Faber, 1960; New York: Humanities Press, 1961; 2nd revised ed., 1962). 'In general the aim of this study, which makes no claim to be comprehensive, is to find some shape in recent theatrical events.'

———. *Drama in the Sixties; Form and Interpretation* (London: Faber and Faber, 1966). Reprinted periodical contributions.

Kronenberger, Louis, ed. 'The London Scene,' *The Best Plays of 1952–61*, 9 vols (New York: Dodd, Mead, 1952–61). An annual survey.

Lahr, John. *Up Against the Fourth Wall; Essays on Modern Theater* (New York: Grove Press, 1970). Includes essays on Harold Pinter and John Osborne.

———. *Astonish Me; Adventures in Contemporary Theater* (New York: Viking Press, 1973). Includes essays on and references to contemporary British playwrights.

Lambert, Jack W. *Drama in Britain, 1964–1973* (Harlow, Essex: Longman for the British Council, 1974). Survey.

Leech, Clifford. 'Two Romantics: Arnold Wesker and Harold Pinter,' *Contemporary Theatre*, ed. John Russell Brown and Bernard Harris, Stratford-upon-Avon Studies, 4 (London: Edward Arnold, 1961; New York: St Martin's Press, 1962).

———. *The Dramatist's Experience; With Other Essays in Literary Theory* (London: Chatto and Windus; New York: Barnes and Noble, 1970). Includes some references to modern British playwrights.

Lorda Alaiz, F. M. *Teatro ingles: De Osborne hasta hoy* (Madrid: Taurus, 1964). Studies of John Osborne, Arnold Wesker, Willis Hall, Frederick Bland, Sam Thomson, Shelagh Delaney, John Arden, Bernard Kops, Harold

Pinter, Ann Jellicoe, N. F. Simpson, Brendan Behan, Nigel Dennis and John Mortimer.

Lumley, Frederick. *Trends in 20th Century Drama: A Survey Since Ibsen and Shaw* (London: Barrie and Rockliff, 1956; revised ed., 1960). Updated and reprinted as *New Trends in 20th Century Drama: A Survey Since Ibsen and Shaw* (London: Barrie and Rockliff; New York: Oxford University Press, 1967). Comprehensive survey.

The Lyric Players 1951–1959 (Belfast: Lyric Players, 1960). Brochure to launch an appeal for financial support.

Lyric Theatre 1951–1968 (Belfast: Lyric Theatre, [1968]). Survey of the famous Theatre in Northern Ireland.

Mabley, Edward. *Dramatic Construction; An Outline of Basic Principles* (Philadelphia: Chilton Book Company, 1972). Analysis of plays by dramatists including Samuel Beckett, Harold Pinter and Robert Bolt.

McCarthy, Mary. *Theatre Chronicles 1937–1962* (New York: Farrar, Straus, 1963). Collected essays and reviews. Much of the material had previously been published as *Sights and Spectacles, 1937–1958* (New York: Farrar, Straus; London: Heinemann, 1959).

McCrindle, Joseph F., ed. *Behind the Scenes: Theater and Film Interviews* (New York: Holt, Rinehart and Winston; London: Pitman, 1971). Includes interviews with Robert Bolt, Peter Shaffer and Tom Stoppard. Reprinted from the *Transatlantic Review*.

Mander, John. *The Writer and Commitment* (London: Secker and Warburg, 1961). Includes chapters on John Osborne and Arnold Wesker.

Marcus, Frank. 'The London Theatre in 1970,' *Theatre 71*, ed. Sheridan Morley (London: Hutchinson, 1971), pp.

9–22. The playwright and drama critic of the *Sunday Telegraph* assesses a reactionary year.

Marowitz, Charles. 'Notes from the Underground,' *Theatre 71*, ed. Sheridan Morley (London: Hutchinson, 1971), pp. 23–32. The founder and artistic director of the Open Space Theatre looks at the past twelve months on the 'fringe.'

———. *Confessions of a Counterfeit Critic; A London Theatre Notebook 1958–1971* (London: Eyre Methuen, 1973). Reprinted reviews.

———, Tom Milne and Owen Hale, eds. *The Encore Reader; A Chronicle of the New Drama*, with a foreword by Richard Findlater (London: Methuen, 1965). Collection of essays and interviews from *Encore.*

———, and Simon Trussler, eds. *Theatre at Work; Playwrights and Productions in the Modern British Theatre*, with an introduction by Irving Wardle (London: Methuen, 1967; New York: Hill and Wang, 1968). A collection of interviews and essays.

Maschler, Tom, ed. *Declaration* (London: MacGibbon and Kee, 1957, New York: E. P. Dutton, 1958). Contributions by Colin Wilson, John Osborne, John Wain, Kenneth Tynan, Bill Hopkins, Lindsay Anderson, Stuart Holroyd and Doris Lessing.

May, Robin, comp. *The Wit of the Theatre*, with a prologue by J. C. Trewin (London: Leslie Frewin, 1969). Selective anthology.

Meloni, Gabrielle. 'I Giovani Arrabbiati E La Dinamica Strutturale Del Teatro Inglese Negli Anni 1956–1963,' *Studi E Ricerche Di Letteratura Inglese E Americana*, vol. 2, ed. Claudio Gorlier (Milano: Cisalpino–Goliardica, 1971), pp. 53–107. Survey.

Merchant, W. Moelwyn. 'Contemporary Trends,' *Creed and Drama; An Essay in Religious Drama* (London: SPCK, 1965), pp. 110–17. Survey.

Morgan, Geoffrey, ed. *Contemporary Theatre; A Selection of Reviews 1966–67* (London: London Magazine Editions, 1968). Reprinted from various British newspapers.

Morley, Sheridan, ed. *Theatre 71* (London: Hutchinson, 1971). Collection of essays; 'the first of a series of annual volumes designed to give a continuing picture of the theatre as it evolves during the 1970's.'

———, ed. *Theatre 72* (London: Hutchinson, 1972).

———, ed. *Theatre 73* (London: Hutchinson, 1973).

———, ed. *Theatre 74* (London: Hutchinson, 1974).

Muir, Kenneth. 'Verse and Prose,' *Contemporary Theatre*, ed. John Russell Brown and Bernard Harris, Stratford-upon-Avon Studies, 4 (London: Edward Arnold, 1962), pp. 97–115. Survey of poetic drama.

Natev, Atanas. *Sovremennaya zapadnaya dramaturgiya* [Contemporary Western Drama] (Moscow: Progress, 1969). Russian translation of Bulgarian original, 1965.

Nathan, George Jean. 'Sample British Imports,' *The Theatre in the Fifties* (New York: Alfred A. Knopf, 1953), pp. 124–60. '. . . a detailed impression of the over-all picture.'

Nicol, Bernard de Bear, ed. 'The British Theatre Now,' *Varieties of Dramatic Experience* (London: University of London Press, 1969). Discussions between Stanley Evernden, Roger Hubank, Thora Burnley Jones and Bernard de Bear Nicol.

Nicoll, Allardyce. *The Theatre and Dramatic Theory*

(London: George G. Harrap, 1962). Includes some references to modern British plays.

———. 'Somewhat In a New Dimension,' *Contemporary Theatre*, ed. John Russell Brown and Bernard Harris, Stratford-upon-Avon Studies, 4 (London: Edward Arnold; New York: St Martin's Press, 1962), pp. 77–95. Comparison between the dramatists of the fifties and those of the Edwardian and Georgian eras.

———. 'The Modern Drama,' *English Drama: A Modern Viewpoint* (London: George G. Harrap, 1968), pp. 126–59. Survey.

O'Casey, Sean. *Blasts and Benedictions; Articles and Stories*, selected and introduced by Ronald Ayling (London: Macmillan; New York: St Martin's Press, 1967). Writings between 1926, when he first came to England, and 1964, the year of his death.

OhAodha, Michael. *The Abbey–Then and Now* (Dublin: Abbey Theatre, 1969). A monograph bringing the Abbey Theatre's history up to 1969.

———. *Theatre in Ireland* (Oxford: Basil Blackwell; Totowa, New Jersey: Rowan and Littlefield, 1974). Traces the formative processes which have shaped Irish drama from the opening of the first theatre in Ireland in 1637 to the reopening of the Gate Theatre, on a subsidised basis, in 1971.

Oppel, Horst, ed. *Das Moderne Englische Drama: Interpretationen* (Berlin: Erich Schmidt, 1963). Includes studies of plays by John Osborne and Arnold Wesker.

Pasquier, Marie-Claire, Nicole Rougier and Bernard Brugiére. *Le nouveau théâtre anglais* (Paris: Armand Colin, 1969). Survey from 1956 to 1968, with chapters on John Osborne, Arnold Wesker, John Arden, and Harold Pinter.

Popkin, Henry, ed. 'Introduction.' *The New British Drama* (New York: Grove Press, 1964), pp. 7–25.

Rafroidi, Patrick, Raymonde Popot and William Parker, eds. *Aspects of the Irish Theatre* (Lille: PUL; Paris: Editions Universitaires, 1972). Anthology of critical articles.

Roberts, James L. 'The Role of Society in the Theater of the Absurd,' *Literature and Society: A Selection of Papers Delivered at the Joint Meeting of the Midwest Modern Language Association and the Central Renaissance Conference, 1963*, ed. Bernice Slote (Lincoln, Nebraska: University of Nebraska Press, 1964), pp. 229–40. Every play in the Theater of the Absurd laughs in anguish at the confusion that exists in contemporary society; 'hence, all share a basic point of view, while varying widely in scope and structure'.

Roberts, Peter. 'New Writing,' *Theatre in Britain; A Playgoer's Guide* (London: Pitman, 1975), pp. 17–26. Survey.

Roy, Emil. 'The Moderns: Osborne, Arden, Pinter, Wesker, and Whiting,' *British Drama Since Shaw* (Carbondale and Edwardsville, Illinois: Southern Illinois University Press; London and Amsterdam: Feffer and Simons, 1972). '. . . finds that no other nation in the world can equal the industry and inventiveness of Britain's living dramatists.'

Salem, Daniel. *La révolution théâtrale actuelle en Angleterre* (Paris: Denöël, 1969). Maps the complete territory of the British theatre for French readers.

Scott, Nathan A., Jr, ed. *The Climate of Faith in Modern Literature* (New York: Seabury Press, 1964), pp. 102–41. Includes two articles: 'Being and Faith in the Contemporary Theater' by Kay Baxter and 'The Christian Presence in the Contemporary Theater' by E. Martin Browne.

Seltzer, Daniel, ed. *The Modern Theatre: Readings and*

Documents (Boston: Little, Brown, 1967). Anthology of articles on various aspects of the theatre.

Shank, Theodore. *The Art of Dramatic Art* (Belmont, California: Dickenson, 1969). 'In this book I have attempted to provide an understanding of dramatic art as a single, unique fine art, distinct from literature and the other arts with which it is sometimes associated.'

Sharp, William L. *Language in Drama; Meanings for the Director and the Actor* (Scranton, Pennsylvania: Chandler, 1970). Makes references to some modern British plays.

Sherek, Henry. 'Playwrights,' *Theatre 1955–6*, ed. Ivor Brown (London: Max Reinhardt, 1956), pp. 140–3. Argues that the essential basis of a healthy theatre is the playwright 'and in this we, in this country, are having a very thin time indeed just now.'

Shestakov, D., ed. 'Introduction,' *Sem' angliiskikh p'es* [Seven English Plays] (Moscow: Iskusstvó, 1968). The plays included are by Shelagh Delaney, Bernard Kops, Brendan Behan, Robert Bolt, John Osborne, Harold Pinter and Arnold Wesker.

———. *Sovremennaya angliyskaya drama (Osbornoucy)* [Contemporary English Drama (The Followers of Osborne)] (Moscow: Vysshaya Shkola, 1968).

Simpson, Alan. *Beckett and Behan and a Theatre in Dublin* (London: Routledge and Kegan Paul, 1962). The Pike Theatre.

Singh, Ram Sewak. *Absurd Drama, 1945–1965* (Delhi: Hariyana Prakashan, 1973).

Smith, R. D. 'Back to the Text' *Contemporary Theatre*, ed. John Russell Brown and Bernard Harris, Stratford-upon-Avon Studies, 4 (London: Edward Arnold, 1961; New

York: St Martin's Press, 1962), pp. 117–38. 'There is so little attention paid to what new playwrights actually write.'

Stanford, Derek, ed. *Landmarks* (London and Camden, New Jersey: Thomas Nelson, 1969). Includes plays, with introductory notes, by Samuel Beckett, John Osborne, Brendan Behan, Shelah Delaney, Arnold Wesker, Harold Pinter, Terence Rattigan, Peter Shaffer, Keith Waterhouse and Willis Hall.

Styan, J. L. 'Television Drama,' *Contemporary Theatre*, ed. John Russell Brown and Bernard Harris, Stratford-upon-Avon, 4 (London: Edward Arnold, 1961; New York: St Martin's 1962), pp. 185–204. Survey.

———. *The Dark Comedy; The Development of Modern Comic Tragedy*, 2nd ed. (Cambridge: Cambridge University Press, 1968). Includes studies of Samuel Beckett and Harold Pinter.

———. *Drama, Stage and Audience* (Cambridge: Cambridge University Press, 1975). Makes illustrations from some contemporary British plays.

Taylor, John Russell. *Anger and After; A Guide to the New British Drama* (London: Methuen, 1962; 2nd revised ed., 1969). The American edition entitled *The Angry Theatre* (New York: Hill and Wang, 1962). Deals with all important contemporary British dramatists.

———. 'British Drama of the Fifties,' *On Contemporary Literature; An Anthology of Critical Essays on the Major Movements and writers of Contemporary Literature*, ed. Richard Kostelanetz (New York: Avon Books, 1964), pp. 90–6. Survey.

———. *The Second Wave; British Drama for the Seventies* (London: Methuen; New York: Hill and Wang, 1971).

Takes up the story of contemporary British drama where his earlier book *Anger and After* left off.

Trewin, J. C. 'Two Morality Playwrights: Robert Bolt and John Whiting,' *Experimental Drama*, ed. William A. Armstrong (London: G. Bell, 1963; New York: Dufour, 1965), pp. 103–27.

———. *Drama in Britain 1951–1964* (London: Longmans, for the British Council, 1965). '. . . discusses the principal strands in the complexity of the British theatre.'

Tynan, Kenneth. 'The British Theatre,' *Curtains* (New York: Atheneum, 1961), pp. 3–244. Reprinted play reviews and essays on general themes.

———. *Tynan on Theatre* (Harmondsworth, Middlesex: Penguin, 1964). A revised selection from *Curtains*.

———. *Tynan Right & Left* (London: Longmans; New York: Atheneum, 1967). Reprinted play reviews and essays.

———. *A View of the English Stage* (London: Davis-Poynter, 1975). Reprinted reviews of performances between 1946 and 1960.

Ungvari, Tamas. *Modern tragikum–tragikus modernseg* [Modern Tragedy–Tragic Modernism] (Budapest: Gondolat, 1966). Includes studies of Samuel Beckett and Arnold Wesker.

Van Zanten, John. *Caught in the Act: Modern Drama as Prelude to the Gospel* (Philadelphia: Westminster Press, 1971). Includes studies of plays by Samuel Beckett and Robert Bolt.

Wager, Walter, ed. *The Playwrights Speak*, with an introduction by Harold Clurman (New York: Delacorte Press,

1967). Includes interviews with John Osborne, Harold Pinter, John Arden and Arnold Wesker.

Ward, A. C. 'Playwrights,' *Twentieth-Century English Literature 1901–1960* (London: Methuen, 1964), pp. 90–142. Survey.

Waterhouse, Keith and Willis Hall, eds. *Writers' Theatre* (London: Heinemann, 1967). The editors 'asked each dramatist to choose his favourite passage from one of his plays, and to make some introductory comments.'

Weise, Wolf-Dietrich. *Die 'neuen englischen Dramatiker' in inhrem Verhältnis zu Brecht* (Bod Homburg: Gehlen, 1969). Includes studies of John Arden, Brendan Behan, Robert Bolt, Shelagh Delaney, John Osborne, Harold Pinter, Peter Schaffer, Arnold Wesker and John Whiting; as well as references to other minor dramatists.

Welland, Dennis. 'Some Post-War Experiments in Poetic Drama,' *Experimental Drama*, ed. William A. Armstrong (London: G. Bell, 1963; New York: Dufour, 1965), pp. 36–55.

Wellwarth, George E. 'The New English Dramatists,' *The Theatre of Protest and Paradox; Developments in the Avant-Grade Drama* (New York: New York University Press; London: MacGibbon and Kee, 1964). pp. 196–273. '. . . suggests that although individual plays may differ radically, they share a common theme–protest–and a common technique–paradox.'

Wesker, Arnold. *Fears of Fragmentation* (London: Jonathan Cape, 1970). Collection of articles.

Whiting, Frank M. 'The Theatre of the Absurd,' *An Introduction to the Theatre*, 3rd ed. (New York and London: Harper and Row, 1969), pp. 139–43. Survey.

Whiting, John. *John Whiting on Theatre*, 'London Magazine' Editions, no. 4 (London: Alan Ross, 1966). Reviews from the *London Magazine.*

———. *The Art of the Dramatist*, ed. with an introduction by Ronald Hayman (London: London Magazine Editions, 1970). Selection of his critical writings.

Wickham, Glynne. *Drama in a World of Science* (London: Routledge and Kegan Paul; Toronto: University of Toronto Press, 1962). Four lectures: 'The Post-War Revolution in British Drama,' 'Poets and Playmakers,' 'Drama in a World of Science' and 'University Theatre.'

Williams, Raymond. 'Recent Drama: Four Plays,' *Drama from Ibsen to Brecht* (London: Chatto and Windus, 1968). By John Whiting, John Osborne, Harold Pinter and John Arden.

———. 'Recent English Drama,' *The Modern Age*, Pelican Guide to English Literature 7, ed. Boris Ford (Harmondsworth, Middlesex: Penguin Books, 1961), pp. 496–508. A revised version of an article originally published in the *Twentieth Century* (London), CLXX (Autumn 1961), 169–80. Reprinted as 'New English Drama,' in *Modern British Dramatists; A Collection of Critical Essays*, ed. John Russell Brown (Englewood Cliffs, New Jersey: Prentice–Hall, 1968). pp. 26–37.

Williamson, Audrey. *Contemporary Theatre, 1953–1956* (London: Rockliff, 1956). Reprinted material from the *Age* and the *Stage.*

Worth, Katharine J. 'Avant Garde at the Royal Court Theatre: John Arden and N. F. Simpson,' *Experimental Drama*, ed. William A. Armstrong (London: G. Bell, 1963; New York: Dufour, 1965), pp. 204–23.

———. *Revolutions in Modern English Drama* (London: G. Bell, 1972; Toronto: Clarke, Irwin, 1973). Chapters on most leading contemporary British dramatists.

Young, B. A. 'The London Theatre,' *Theatre 72*, ed. Sheridan Morley (London: Hutchinson, 1972), pp. 11–27. The drama critic and arts editor of the *Financial Times* looks back over a farcical year.

———. 'The West End: 1973–4,' *Theatre 74*, ed. Sheridan Morley (London: Hutchinson, 1974), pp. 38–48. The drama critic and arts editor of the *Financial Times* surveys the year in the commercial theatre.

Periodical Articles

Abirached, Robert. 'Le jeune théâtre anglais,' *Nouvelle Revue Française*, XV (February 1967), 314–21. Examines plays by James Saunders, John Osborne, Ann Jellicoe, Harold Pinter and John Arden.

Alisoun, Swete. [Editorial], *The Times Literary Supplement* (London) (25 January 1957), p. 49. The decline of the hero in modern drama.

Alvarez, A. 'The Anti-Establishment Drama,' *Partisan Review*, XXVI (Fall 1959), 606–11. '. . . in the late 'fifties, the audience is much the same but the middle-class image of itself, its known facts and willed fantasies, have changed.'

Amette, Jacques-Pierre. 'Osborne, Pinter, Saunders & Cie,' *Nouvelle Revue Française*, XVIII (January 1970), 95–9. Observations.

Andersen, Jorgen. 'Englaendere i repertoiret,' *Perspektiv* (Copenhagen), X, no. 1 (1962), 45–52. Survey of the 1950s and the 1960s.

Anderson, Michael. 'Edinburgh,' *Plays and Players* (London), XX, no. 1 (October 1972), 54–5; XX, no. 2 (November 1972), 50–1. Survey of Edinburgh Festival drama offerings.

Andrews, Nigel. 'Lunch & Late Night Line-Up,' *Plays and Players* (London), XVIII, no. 3 (December 1970), 50. Survey of lunchtime and late-night shows.

————. 'Lunch Line-Up,' *Plays and Players* (London), XVIII, no. 11 (August 1971), 51. Survey of lunchtime theatres.

Angus, William. 'Modern Theatre Reflects the Times,' *Queen's Quarterly*, LXX (1963), 255–63. 'There is a marked increase in the amount of frenetic, high-strung anxiety and instability.'

Anikst, A. 'Ot Osborna k Merseru: Sotsial'nye problemy v sovremennoi angliiskoi drame [From Osborne to Mercer: Social Problems in English Drama],' *Teatr* (Moscow), VI (1969), 147–57.

Ansorge, Peter. 'All Our Yesterdays–1956,' *Plays and Players* (London), XIV, no. 2 (November 1966), 66–7. On the year in which *Look Back in Anger* opened and the Berliner Ensemble arrived in London.

————. 'Ireland,' *Plays and Players* (London), XV, no. 8 (May 1968), 60–2. On the Abbey Theatre's offering at the World Theatre Season in London.

————. 'Underground Explorations–No. 1: Portable Playwrights,' *Plays and Players* (London), XIX, no. 5 (February 1972), 14–23. Interviews with Howard Brenton, David Hare, Malcolm Griffiths and Snoo Wilson.

———— 'Underground Explorations,' *Plays and Players* (London), XIX, no. 6 (March 1972), 18–24; no. 7 (April 1972), 14–18; no. 8 (May 1972), 14–17; no. 9 (June 1972), 12–14, 59. Survey.

———. 'Current Concerns,' *Plays and Players* (London), XXI, no. 10 (July 1974), 18–22. Trevor Griffiths and David Hare outline the problems of two contemporary playwrights in an interview.

Archer, Kane. 'What Really Happened,' *Plays and Players* (London), XXII, no. 3 (December 1974). 32–4. Survey of Dublin Theatre Festival.

Arden, John. 'Theatre Survey: New Authors–Visitors at the Court,' *Encore* (London) (September 1958), 37–9. The season of visiting Repertory Companies to the Royal Court Theatre, London.

———. 'A Thoroughly Romantic View,' *London Magazine*, VII (July 1960), 11–15. Mainly on the Royal Court Theatre.

———. 'Tatty Theatre,' *Guardian* (London) (16 May 1964), p. 14. Not enough time is given to productions.

Armstrong, William A. 'Modern Developments in the British Theatre,' *Neuphilologische Mitteilungen*, LI (February 1950), 19–34. Survey.

———. 'Tradition and Innovation in the London Theatre, 1960–61,' *Modern Drama*, IV, no. 2 (September 1961), 184–95. Survey.

Arnold, Sidney. 'The Abbey Theatre,' *Arts and Philosophy* (London), I (Summer 1950), 25–30. 'It is as yet as an infant that is nearer to Homer rather than an adolescent who is ignorant of the soul of the poet.'

Arup, Jens. 'The English Repertory Theatre Today,' *Listener* (London), LXIII (28 January 1960), 168–70. Considers the influence of repertories on the West End.

Ashmore, Jerome. 'Interdisciplinary Roots of the Theatre of the Absurd,' *Modern Drama,* XIV (May 1971), 72–83. Considers the scope of the absurd and the variety of its manifestations.

Ashworth, Arthur. 'New Theatre: Ionesco, Beckett, Pinter,' *Southerly* (Sydney), XXII, no. 3 (1962), 145–54. 'Plot, character and dialogue are so treated that from the realistic viewpoint they are fantastic.'

'At Last,' *Drama* (London), no. 66 (Autumn 1962), 17. The announcement on 4 July that a National Theatre is at last to be built.

Atkins, Thomas R. 'The London Theater: A Devaluation,' *Kenyon Review,* XXXI, no. 3 (1969), 348–66. 'London is not the theatrical center of the Western World.'

Atkinson, Brooks. 'Britain's Ritual Molds Her Theatre,' *New York Times Magazine* (24 July 1955), pp. 16, 40. 'The London stage has deep roots in the British character. Its acting has formality and design.'

'Au Revoir to the Abbey Theatre,' *Sunday Times* (London) (25 January 1959), p. 9. To preserve a record of the Abbey Theatre before it was pulled down for rebuilding, some of its former illustrious members visited it to make a film.

'Authors,' *Twentieth Century* (London), CLXIX (February 1961), 151–2. Brief survey of contemporary British drama.

'Back to the Wooden O?' *The Economist,* CCI (7 October 1961), 31–2. On the provincial theatre.

Bakewell, Michael. 'The Producer and the Television Play,' *Listener* (London), LXXVI (7 July 1966), 9–10. 'The role of the television producer in today's television drama might fairly be compared to that of an old-style impresario.'

Barfoot, C. C. 'New Poems, New Plays: An Annual Survey,' *Dutch Quarterly Review of Anglo-American Letters*, I (1971), 15–26. Survey of plays and collections of plays published in 1969.

Barker, Clive. 'The State of the British Theatre,' *Views*, no. 5 (Summer 1964), 93–9. Deals with the basic problems facing the British theatre today from the viewpoint of the artist.

———. 'Contemporary Shakespearean Parody in British Theatre,' *Shakespeare-Jahrbuch* (Weimar), CV (1969), 104–20. Considers some contemporary plays which reflect both positive and negative aspects of a changing attitude towards Shakespeare.

Barker, Ronald. 'The London Scene,' *Plays and Players* (London), I, no. 1 (October 1953), 7. Survey.

Barnes, Clive. 'England's National Theatre,' *Nation* (New York), CXCVII (7 December 1963), 399–400.

———. 'West End Story,' *Saturday Review*, LIII (12 September 1970), 52–4.

Barnet, David. 'The Future for Television Drama,' *Twentieth Century* (London), CLXXV (Autumn 1966), 46–8. '. . . there can be an original form owing nothing directly to the cinema or the theatre.'

Bastable, Adolphus. 'Our Theatres in the Sixties,' *Shavian*, III, no. 2 (1966), 14–18. Survey.

———. 'Our Theatres in the Sixties,' *Shavian*, III, no. 8 (1967), 17–22. Survey.

Becker, William. 'English Theatre: A Budding Tradition,' *New Republic,* CXXIX (21 September 1953), 19–20. On Old Vic and Stratford.

'Becoming a Dramatist,' *Plays and Players* (London), XIII, no. 4 (January 1966), 52–6. Simon Trussler in England and Gerald Colgan in Ireland talk to a cross-section of playwrights at the start of their careers.

Benvenisti, J. L. 'The Play's the Thing,' *Commonweal,* LXXI (20 November 1959), 237–9. On the British repertory movement.

Bernhard, F. J. 'English Theater 1963: In the Wake of the New Wave,' *Books Abroad,* XXXVIII (Spring 1964), 143–4.

'Better Dead,' *Plays and Players* (London), V, no. 5 (February 1958), 22. On censorship.

'The Big Row Over Dirty Plays,' *Time and Tide* (London), XLV (3 September 1964), 10–12. Summary of the row at the Theatre Royal, Drury Lane.

Billington, Michael. 'A Question of Colour,' *Plays and Players* (London), XIII, no. 1 (October 1965), 8–12. Investigates the opportunities for coloured artists in the English Theatre.

———. 'London Avant Garde: Who? What? Where?' *Plays and Players* (London), XVII, no. 9 (June 1970), 20–1. 'There is no one word that adequately sums up the whole range of new activities that sprang up in London over the last few years.'

———. 'Lunch & Late Night Line-Up,' *Plays and Players* (London), XVII, no. 11 (August 1970), 51. Survey of lunchtime and late-night shows in London.

———. 'Edinburgh,' *Plays and Players* (London), XVIII, no. 1 (October 1970), 40–55. Survey of Edinburgh Festival drama offerings.

'The Biter Bit,' *Plays and Players* (London), VIII, no. 6 (March 1961), 20. Editorial defending the new dramatists.

Blumenfeld, Yorick. 'The London Show,' *Atlantic*, CCXXIV (August 1969), 99–101. 'The playwrights on the West End . . . seem to believe that they must intentionally distort history as a provocation for their presumably upper-class audiences.'

Boas, Guy. 'Professionals and Amateurs,' *Drama* (London), no. 61 (Winter 1962), 29–31. '. . . not infrequently the amateur . . . will give you everything which you want to perfection.'

———. 'The Theatre of Cruelty,' *Drama* (London), no. 73 (Winter 1964), 29–32. The influence of Artaud on the contemporary English theatre.

Bolt, Robert. 'English Theatre Today: The Importance of Shape,' *International Theatre Annual*, III (1957–8), 140–5. 'I will put down one after another the things I do seem to believe about the Theatre.'

Bond, Edward. 'Millstones Round the Playwright's Neck,' *Plays and Players* (London), XIII, no. 7 (April 1966), 70. An author's view of critics.

'The Boom in Britain,' *Time*, LXV (9 May 1955), 91.

Bourque, Joseph H. 'Theatre of the Absurd: A New Approach to Audience Reaction,' *Research Studies of Washington State University*, XXXV (December 1968), 311–24. Shows that the Theatre of the Absurd seeks a new kind of audience reaction by engaging the emotions and the senses rather than the intellect of the spectator.

Bowen, John. 'The Fashion Makers,' *Encore* (London) (September 1960). 28–34. On the responsibilities of the reviewer.

———. 'Accepting the Illusion,' *Twentieth Century* (London), CLXIX (February 1961), 153–65. Takes a fresh look at the labels 'realism' and 'naturalism' in relation to contemporary writing for the theatre and TV.

———. 'Is Television Drama Dead?' *Listener* (London), LXXI (16 April 1964), 624, 627, 629. Observations by a writer of television plays.

Bowers, Faubion. 'Theatre of the Absurd: It Is Here to Stay,' *Theatre Arts* (New York), XLVI (November 1962), 21, 23–4, 64. Observations.

Bowker, Gordon. 'Paddy, Taffie and Jock,' *Plays and Players* (London), XIV, no. 2 (November 1966), 62–5. On nationalism and the theatre.

Brabazon, James. 'Surveying the London Theater: New Liberties Bear Fruit,' *Christian Century*, LXXXIX (26 April 1972), 490–1.

Bradley, Jeana. 'London Stages, 1961,' *Westerly*, I (November 1962), 111–14. Survey by an Australian.

Brahms, Caryl. 'Theatre '61,' *Plays and Players* (London), IX, no. 4 (January 1962), 8. Survey of 'the past twelve months in the theatre.'

———. 'A Season of Playgoing,' *Dublin Review*, no. 507 (Spring 1966), 79–90. 'This season has been the beginning of a Renaissance in the London Theatre.'

———. 'Today's Theatre of Disenchanted Classless Writers,' *The Times* (London) (18 April 1968), p. 9. Comparison between the thirties and now.

Brandt, G. W. 'The Domestic Playwright: Some Thoughts about Television Drama,' *A Review of English Literature,* III, no. 4 (October 1962), 17–28. On drama transmitted by BBC and ITV.

Brien, Alan. 'Critic's Choice: The London Season,' *Theatre Arts* (New York), XLIII (May 1959), 9–15, 72. Survey by the drama critic of the *Sunday Telegraph.*

———. 'Theatre, London,' *Theatre Arts* (New York), XLIII (December 1959), 20–5. Survey.

———. 'London: City in a State of Flux,' *Theatre Arts* (New York), XLIV (April 1960), 14–16, 64–5. 'The British theatre is momentarily in the melting pot.'

———. 'London Lights Are All Aglow,' *Theatre Arts* (New York), XLV (February 1961), 59–60, 76. Survey.

———. 'The London Scene,' *Theatre Arts* (New York), XLVI (January 1962), 64–7. Survey.

———. 'London's Season: The Latest Plays,' *Theatre Arts* (New York), XLVI (May 1962), 24–6. Survey.

———. 'Openings,' *Theatre Arts* (New York), XLVI (December 1962), 57–9. Survey.

———. 'Openings,' *Theatre Arts* (New York), XLVII (January 1963), 57–9, 70–3. Survey.

———. 'Arrogance Please,' *Plays and Players* (London), X, no. 5 (February 1963), 12–13. On the responsibilities of the drama critic.

Brine, Adrian. 'Challenge on Home Ground,' *Drama* (London), no. 45 (Summer 1957), 33–4.

———. 'The Translation Scandal,' *Plays and Players*

(London), XIII, no. 11 (August 1966), 50–1. 'Many English directors working abroad do not realise how their work is being unwittingly undermined by inaccurate or unspeakable texts.'

———. 'Get the Guests,' *Plays and Players* (London), XIV, no. 6 (March 1967), 62–3. On the Audience's changing status.

'Brisk Business Behind the Box-Office,' *Time and Tide* (London) (7–13 November 1963), p. 34.

'The British Drama League,' *Drama* (London), no. 46 (Autumn 1957), 17. Menaced by the ever-rising costs of administration.

'British Play Writing,' *Encore* (London) (June 1957), pp. 13–35. Full text of the discussion held at the Royal Court Theatre, 18 November 1956. Chairman: Kenneth Tynan. Panel: Benn W. Levy, Wolf Mankowitz, Arthur Miller, John Whiting and Colin Wilson.

Brook, Peter. 'The Contemporary Theatre; The Vitality of the English Stage,' *Listener* (London) (4 May 1950), pp. 781–2.

Brooke, Nicholas. 'The Characters of Drama,' *Critical Quarterly*, VI (1964), 72–82. The best 'serious' drama of late has been strongly rooted in theatrical entertainment rather than in the 'straight play' 'conflict of characters' tradition.

Brosnan, Gerald. 'Dublin's Abbey–the Immortal Theatre,' *Theatre Arts* (New York), XXXV, no. 10 (October 1951), 36–7. Recollections by a playwright who happened to be in Dublin and to see the ruins of the Abbey Theatre, which went up in flames on 18 July 1951.

Brown, Ivor. 'Troubles of the Time,' *Drama* (London), no. 36

(Spring 1955), 21–3. 'The London theatres get clogged up with the Show Business productions and also with long-running rough-and-tumble comedies.'

———. 'The Best of 1955,' *Plays and Players* (London), III, no. 3 (December 1955), 10–11. About 'the plays and performances that have most impressed him during the past year.'

———. 'The Press and the Theatre,' *Drama* (London), no. 44 (Spring 1957), 30–2. '. . . dramatic criticism dwindles while theatre gossip and "stories of the Stars" increase.'

———. 'Forty Years Back,' *Drama* (London), no. 52 (Spring 1959), 25–7. A balance-sheet of theatrical gains and losses during the forty years since the British Drama League was founded.

———. 'From Blood to Mud,' *Drama* (London), no. 55 (Winter 1959), 29–31. 'The theatre of today . . . has its own excess of ugliness.'

———. 'Theatre, Press and Public,' *Drama* (London), no. 59 (Winter 1960), 28–30. Comparison between dramatic criticism now and forty years ago.

———. 'The New Bardolatry,' *Drama* (London), no. 64 (Spring 1962), 34–6. 'Bardolatry flourishes as it certainly did not between the wars.'

———. 'Dramatic Approaches,' *Plays and Players* (London), X, no. 2 (November 1962), 47. Review article.

———. 'Gas-Bag's Paradise,' *Drama* (London), no. 68 (Spring 1963), 28–30. '. . . the drama is more argued and written about than the other arts.'

———. 'Stage and Status,' *Plays and Players* (London), XIII, no. 5 (February 1966), 62. On the actor's changing status in society.

———. 'The High Froth,' *Drama* (London), no. 87 (Winter 1967), 32–4. 'Among the rarest things in the English theatre of today is a fine flow of words.'

———. 'All Mixed Up,' *Drama* (London), no. 97 (Summer 1970), 43–5. 'The theatre, with or without partition by a curtain, is a great mixer.'

———. 'The Real Thing,' *Drama* (London), no. 105 (Summer 1972), 42–5. Comparison between realism in the contemporary theatre and in the Edwardian and Georgian theatre.

Browne, E. Martin. 'Religious Drama Since 1939,' *The National and English Review*, (March 1952), pp. 160–2. Survey.

———. 'A Look Round the English Theatre, 1961,' *Drama Survey,* I (1961), 227–31. Survey.

———. 'A Look Round the English Theatre, Summer, 1964,' *Drama Survey,* IV (Spring 1965), 70–5. Survey.

———. 'A First Look Round the English Theatre, 1965,' *Drama Survey,* IV (Summer 1965), 177–82. Survey.

———. 'A Look Round the English Theatre, Summer and Fall, 1965,' *Drama Survey,* IV (Winter 1965), 272–6. Survey.

———. 'A Look Round the London Theatre, Winter 1965–66,' *Drama Survey,* V (Spring 1966), 87–91. Survey.

———. 'A Look Round the English Theatre, Spring 1966,' *Drama Survey,* V (Summer 1966), 192–6. Survey.

———. 'A Look Round the English Theatre: Summer and Fall, 1966,' *Drama Survey*, V (Winter 1966), 292–9. Survey.

———. 'English Theatre, Winter 1966–67,' *Drama Survey*, VI (Spring 1967), 81–7. Survey.

———. 'English Theatre, Spring-Summer 1967,' *Drama Survey*, VI (Fall 1967), 221–8. Survey.

———. 'English Theatre, Winter 1967–68,' *Drama Survey*, VI (Spring 1968), 311–15. 'A creditable number of new plays of real interest.'

———. 'A Look Around the English Theatre: February May 1968,' *Drama Survey*, VII (Winter 1968), 138–48. The period has produced no major new play.

———. 'A Last Look Round the English Theatre,' *Comparative Drama*, III (Spring 1969), 133–42. Survey.

Brustein, Robert. 'Theater in London,' *New Republic*, CLII (29 May 1965), 30–3, '. . . flatulent British revues; sleek musicals from America; and half-hearted comedy-dramas.'

———. 'The New English Stage,' *New Statesman* (London), LXX (6 August 1965), 193–4. Reprinted as 'The English Stage,' *Modern British Dramatists; A Collection of Critical Essays*, ed. John Russell Brown (Englewood Cliffs, New Jersey: Prentice-Hall, 1968), pp. 164–70. Survey.

———. 'The English Stage,' *Tulane Drama Review*, X, no. 3 (Spring 1966), 127–33. As a movement, the new English drama appears to be temporarily stalled.

———. 'Art in an Age of Ideology,' *New Republic*, CLXVII (28 October 1972), 28–9. '. . . the minds of serious theater people here are preoccupied largely with the Irish question.'

———. 'Repertory Theatre in the Doldrums,' *New Republic*, CLXVII (18 November 1972), 26–7. '. . . for all its apparent health and vigor . . . the English repertory movement seems . . . to have become momentarily stalled.'

Bryden, Ronald. 'Author's Theatre,' *New Statesman* (London), LXVII (27 March 1964), 498–9. On the function of a national theatre.

———. 'Fulfilments,' *New Statesman* (London), LXX (31 December 1965), 1037–8.

———. 'Why Theatres?' *Observer* (London) (14 January 1968), p. 8. On the conflict between the provincial theatre director and the eccentricities of local opinion.

Buckle, Richard. 'Comedy in 1953,' *Plays and Players* (London), I, no. 1 (October 1953), 8–9. Survey.

Burdick, Dolores M. 'The Moral Function of "Immoral" Theatre,' *Performing Arts Review*, I, no. 3 (1970), 445–51. Considers what we mean by decadence in the theatre.

Burrowes, Wesley. 'Writers Are Not Encouraged,' *Irish Times* (Dublin) (18 March 1968), p. 10. There is nothing in Ireland 'to encourage anybody to write a play, except his own dedication.'

Buylla, Jose Benito. 'El teatro de absurdo y su proyeccion Britanica,' *Archivum* (Oviedo, Spain), XVI (1966), 223–43. On the development of the Theatre of the Absurd in Britain.

Byrne, John Keyes. 'Dublin,' *Plays and Players* (London), IV, no. 4 (January 1957), 32, no. 5 (February 1957), 33, no. 6 (March 1957), 32, no. 7 (April 1957), 32, no. 8 (May 1957), 32; V, no. 3 (December 1957), 33, no. 4 (January 1958), 32, no. 5 (February 1958), 33, no. 7 (April 1958),

32, no. 10 (July 1958), 32, no. 11 (August 1958), 32; VI, no. 6 (March 1959), 33, no. 8 (May 1959), 32, no. 9 (June 1959), 32. Survey.

———. 'Clean, If Not Clever,' *Plays and Players* (London), VII, no. 2 (November 1959), 9. Survey of Dublin Festival drama productions.

Caine, Cindy S. A. M. 'Structure in the One-Act Play,' *Modern Drama,* XII, no. 4 (February 1970), 390–8. '. . . today's one-acter seems at most to be in a process of evolution, tending towards a decision of classical form into two major components: the tension line and individual sections.'

Callen, Anthony. 'Stoppard's Godot: Some French Influences on Post-War English Drama,' *New Theatre Magazine,* X, no. 1 (Winter 1969), 22–30. Deals with N. F. Simpson, Harold Pinter and Tom Stoppard.

Caputi, Anthony. 'The Shallows of Modern Serious Drama,' *Modern Drama,* IV, no. 2 (September, 1961), 111–16. 'The staggering majority of serious plays in our time are just such sad songs of self-pity.'

Carroll, Donald. 'Contemporary Irish Theatre,' *Drama* (London), no. 66 (Autumn 1962), 34–6. '. . . the situation does not invite enthusiasm.'

Carroll, Paul Vincent. 'Can the Abbey Theatre Be Restored?' *Theatre Arts* (New York), XXXVI, no. 1 (January 1952), 18–19, 79. The Abbey Theatre has been 'in retreat' as a result of: 1. 'unofficial interference of the Government' 2. 'very powerful unofficial clerical censorship' 3. 'deplorable policy of the Abbey Directorate.'

Champlin, C. D. 'How Beastly Are the British?' *Life,* LVII (6 November 1964), 15. 'This has been the year of the Great London Dirty Play Controversy.'

Churchill, Caryl. 'Not Ordinary, Not Safe; A Direction for Drama?' *Twentieth Century* (London), CLXVIII (November 1960), 443–51. '. . . the fifties seem to have been excited simply by discovering the working man in his kitchen and think he is enough in himself.'

'Classics Eclipsed,' *Plays and Players* (London), VI, no. 11 (August 1959), 20. Editorial urging the West End to offer 'a choice of the best plays of several periods.'

'Clean-up Theatre Demands Grow,' *Time and Tide* (London), XLV (27 August 1964), 10–11. Surveys 'the trend towards plays that are unsuitable and unacceptable to a large part of the public.'

Clurman, Harold. 'Theater,' *Nation* (New York), CLXXVII (15 August 1953), 137–9. 'The English theater today is a theater of actors and old plays.'

———. 'Theater,' *Nation* (New York), CLXXIX (14 August 1954), 138–9. 'The theater in England is regarded in the main as a gentle art.'

———. 'Theater,' *Nation* (New York), CLXXXV (6 July 1957), 17–19. 'Most of the recommended plays in London are foreign.'

———. 'The Theatre,' *Nation* (New York), CLXXXVIII (16 May 1959), 461–3. Three successful plays representing 'three aspects of the English theatre today.'

———. 'Theatre,' *Nation* (New York), CLXXXVIII (30 May 1959), 502–3. The Royal Court Theatre 'is once again the site of important activities.'

———. 'Theatre,' *Nation* (New York), CXCI (20 August 1960), 98–9. The most striking development is the avant garde.

———. 'Theatre,' *Nation* (New York), CXCIII (1 July 1961), 17–19. 'Ever since 1956, there has been an increasing proletarianisation of the English theatre.'

———. 'Theatre,' *Nation* (New York), CXCIV (2 June 1962), 501–2. 'Examined separately, the blossoms of the London bouquet are not unfailingly charming.'

———. 'Theatre,' *Nation* (New York), CXCVI (25 May 1963), 450–2. '. . . the English theatre is enjoying a seizure of satire.'

———. 'Theatre,' *Nation* (New York), CXCVII (19 October 1963), 244–6. The British stage has developed since the mid-fifties.

———. 'Great Britain's National,' *Nation* (New York), CIC (13 July 1964), 18–20. On the first ten plays presented.

———. 'Notes from Afar,' *Nation* (New York), CCI (30 August 1965), 105–6. 'What is missing in so many of the new plays is the substance of experience.'

———. 'The Subject Is Not Roses, or The Grandeur and Misery of Repertory,' *Theatre,* II (1965), 111–21. Deals with the British National Theatre and other repertory companies.

———. 'Theatre,' *Nation* (New York), CCXI (6 July 1970), 28–30.

———. 'Theatre,' *Nation* (New York), CCXI (21 September 1970), 252–3.

———. 'Theatre,' *Nation* (New York), CCXIII (19 July 1971), 61–2.

———. 'Theatre,' *Nation* (New York), CCXIII (27 September 1971), 282–4.

Cohn, Ruby. 'Taking the Drama Seriously,' *Southern Review*, II (Winter 1966), 229–41. Review article.

Coleman, Terry. 'Censorship,' *Guardian* (London) (23 February 1968), p. 8. George Strauss's Bill to abolish theatre censorship comes before the Commons.

Colgan, Gerald. 'Ibsen, Joyce and Kafka,' *Plays and Players* (London), IX, no. 2 (November 1961), 9. Survey of the Dublin Theatre Festival.

———. 'Threadbare Harlequin,' *Plays and Players* (London), X, no. 5 (February 1963) 20–4. Tells how a small group have fought to keep the Dublin theatre alive outside the brief and giddy fortnight of the subsidised Theatre Festival.

———. 'Dublin 1964,' *Plays and Players* (London), XII, no. 1 (October 1964), 11–12. Review of Dublin Theatre Festival.

———. 'Dublin: Second Festival Week,' *Plays and Players* (London), XII, no. 3 (December 1964), 18. Survey.

———. 'Dublin 1965,' *Plays and Players* (London), XIII, no. 1 (October 1965), 15. Survey of Dublin Theatre Festival.

———. 'Dublin Theatre Festival,' *Plays and Players* (London), XIV, no. 1 (October 1966), 54. Looks at the preparations for the Festival.

———. 'Dublin Review,' *Plays and Players* (London), XV, no. 1 (October 1967), 43. Looks ahead to the Dublin Theatre Festival.

———. 'Operation Survival,' *Plays and Players* (London), XV, no. 3 (December 1967), 50, 58. Survey of the 1966 Dublin Theatre Festival.

———. 'Dublin,' *Plays and Players* (London), IX, no. 5 (February 1962), 27, no. 6 (March 1962), 27, no. 7 (April 1962), 27–8, no. 9 (June 1962), 44, no. 10 (July 1962), 48; XVI, no. 1 (October 1968), 66, no. 3 (December 1968), 62–4, no. 6 (March 1969), 46–7, no. 8 (May 1969), 57–8; XVII, no. 3 (December 1969), 52–4, no. 9 (June 1970), 56–7; XVIII, no. 3 (December 1970), 56, no. 6 (March 1971), 58, no. 8 (May 1971), 52–3; XIX, no. 6 (March 1972), 56, no. 8 (May 1972), 38–40; XX, no. 8 (May 1973), 62–3, no. 9 (June 1973), 65; XXI, no. 3 (December 1973), 62–4. Survey.

Collins, Philip. 'Reps,' *London Magazine*, V (August 1965), 67–70. Survey of the repertory theatre.

Colum, Padraic. 'Theatre: Dublin,' *Theatre Arts* (New York). XLVI, no. 2 (February 1960), 24–5. Survey underlining 'the necessity for the opening of a regular national theatre.'

Conolly, L. W. 'The Abolition of Theatre Censorship in Great Britain: The Theatres Act of 1968,' *Queen's Quarterly*, LXXV (1968), 569–83. Survey of the function which had been exercised by the Lord Chamberlain since 1737.

'Contemporary Theatre: Some Theories and Trends,' *Kansas Quarterly*, III (Spring 1971), 3–128. Includes articles on Harold Pinter and Peter Shaffer.

Corbett, James. 'Theatre Workshop: A British People's Theatre,' *Meanjin*, XVIII (September 1959), 327–33. '. . . the Theatre Workshop company of the Theatre Royal, Stratford, believes that drama becomes a life-enhancing force when coupled with the hopes and problems of ordinary people.'

Coughlan, Robert. 'Why Britain's Angry Young Men Boil Over,' *Life*, XLIV (26 May 1958), 138–50. The Angry Young Men have 'so far contributed little in the way of major writing,' but they represent the decreasing feeling for the common good and increasing class and individual responsibility in the declining British Empire.

'Court Jester,' *Plays and Players* (London), V, no. 6 (March 1958), 22. On censorship.

Coveney, Michael. 'Pushing on to a National Theatre,' *Plays and Players* (London), XXI, no. 7 (April 1974), 27–31. Survey of the Theatre in Scotland.

Cox, Frank. 'London's Little Theatres,' *Plays and Players* (London), XII, no. 4 (January 1965), 13–15. 'Facts there are in plenty to justify the existence' of little theatres.

———. 'Two Cheers for Mr. Diarmand,' *Plays and Players* (London), XIV, no. 2 (November 1966), 48–51. Survey of the 1966 Edinburgh drama offerings.

———. 'Writing for the Stage,' *Plays and Players* (London), XIV, no. 12 (September 1967), 40–2, 50. Interview with Keith Dewhurst, Peter Nichols and David Storey.

———. 'Commercial Theatre–Can It Survive?' *Plays and Players* (London), XVII, no. 9 (June 1970), 18–19, 56. London's commercial theatre is experiencing a difficult period economically and aesthetically.

Coxe, Louis. 'Letter from Dublin,' *Nation* (New York), CXC, no. 13 (26 March 1960), 282. 'I have seen little Irish drama, new or old, that I would call really good.'

Craig, Gordon. 'The English Theatre Today,' *Drama* (London), no. 41 (Summer 1956), 30–1. Impressions of the present state of the English theatre.

Cregan, David. 'Reflections about a State Theatre,' *Contemporary Review*, CCXIX (August 1971), 67–72.

'Critic's Choice,' *Plays and Players* (London), IX, no. 8 (May 1926), 7. Editorial on theatre critics.

'Cruelty to Theatregoers?' *The Economist*, CCXIII (12 December 1964), 1254–5. On finance and ticket agencies.

Cusack, Cyril. 'In Terms of Theatre,' *Iris Hibernia* (Fribourg, Switzerland), IV, no. 3 (1960), 20–6. Comments on the Irish theatre past and present.

Cusack, Dymphna. 'The English Theatre,' *Meanjin*, IX (Autumn 1950), 36–8. 'The London stage seems to be given up to the actor and the producer.'

———. 'What Is Wrong with the English Playwright?' *Meanjin*, IX (Winter 1950), 127–30, '. . . the English playwright has no intelligible coherent view of the contemporary world.'

Dallas, Ian. 'Theatre Survey: New Authors–The Naturalists,' *Encore* (London), (September 1958), pp. 24–8. 'A crop of new naturalist playwrights has arisen during the past couple of years.'

Daniels, Vivian A. 'Television and the Playwright,' *Guardian* (London) (5 January 1961), p. 6. Review article.

Darcante, Jean. 'Landmarks in the History of the International Theatre Institute,' *World Theatre*, VIII (Spring 1959), 3–8. Results and growth of the ITI since the venture began a decade ago show that the aim for a world theatre to promote international understanding is nearing fruition.

Darlington, W. A. 'Hits from Britain,' *New York Times Magazine* (17 September 1950), pp. 26–7. '. . . an invasion of Broadway this season by plays which have been notably successful in London.'

———. 'How To Get a Job Without Really Trying,' *Plays and Players* (London), X, no. 8 (May 1963), 20–1. Draws attention to the haphazard way theatre critics come to get their jobs.

———. 'The Message in the Porridge,' *Daily Telegraph* (London) (3 April 1972), p. 5. On censorship.

———. 'Unrepentant Moderate,' *Daily Telegraph* (London) (1 May 1972), p. 11. On censorship.

———. See also his regular contributions to *Daily Telegraph* (London), 1920–68, and the *New York Times*, 1939–60.

Davie, Donald. 'The Dublin Theatre Festival,' *Twentieth Century* (London), CLXII (July 1957), 71–3. Survey of Dublin's first Theatre Festival.

Davis, Malcolm McTear. 'Editor's Report: Lively London,' *Travel*, CXXXI (February 1969), 14. On BOAC's London Show Tours.

Dawson, Helen. 'To Strip or Not To Strip,' *Plays and Players* (London), XVIII, no. 2 (November 1970), 26–8. On nudity in the theatre.

Day-Lewis, Sean. 'Quarter,' *Drama* (London), no. 91 (Winter 1968), 44–7; no. 92 (Spring 1969), 40–2; no. 93 (Summer 1969), 50–3; no. 94 (Autumn 1969), 47–9; no. 95 (Winter 1969), 71–3; no. 96 (Spring 1970), 54–7; no. 97 (Summer 1970), 62–4. Survey.

Dean, Basil. 'Crisis in the Theatre,' *Manchester Guardian* (12 July 1957), p. 8; (13 July 1957), p. 4. I. 'Plays without Patrons'. II. 'The Repertories'.

De Gruyter, Dom. 'Toneel in Engeland,' *Nieuw Vlaams*

Tijdschrift (June 1952), 1089–1106. Survey of the theatre in England.

Dennis, Nigel. 'Speaking of Books: Novelist on Stage,' *New York Times Book Review* (6 November 1966), pp. 2, 62. On differences between a play and a novel.

Dent, Alan. 'Two on the London Aisle,' *Saturday Review*, XL (19 October 1957), 50–1. Comparison between theatre-going in London and in New York.

———. 'The Best Plays and Players of 1960,' *Plays and Players* (London), VIII, no. 4 (January 1961), 4–5. Surveys 'The plays and players that have most impressed him over the last twelve months.'

'Deprive and Corrupt,' *Times Literary Supplement* (16 March 1967), p. 219. The Lord Chamberlain's severity has relaxed over the past few years.

Dews, Peter. 'Theatre–National and Provincial,' *Critical Quarterly,* II (Winter 1960), 355–9. 'A truly National Theatre cannot exist without a healthy provincial one.'

Dobrée, Bonamy. 'Drama in England,' *Sewanee Review*, LXIV (Summer 1956), 470–84. 'Not "English Drama"; for at the moment the theater in London is a pallid patient, kept alive by brisk frequent injections of foreign plays.'

———. 'The London Theater, 1957: The Melting Pot,' *Sewanee Review*, LXVI (Winter 1958), 146–60. Review article.

———. 'The London Stage,' *Sewanee Review*, LXVII (Winter 1959), 109–17. Review article.

Donahue, Francis. 'Anatomy of the "New Drama",' *Southwest Review*, LVI (Summer 1971), 269–77. 'Today, with the 1960s past and the 1970s well begun, the "New Drama" stands defiantly, left of center, on the world's stage.'

Donoghue, Denis. 'Dublin Letter,' *Hudson Review*, XIII, no. 4 (Winter 1960), 579–85. Survey.

———. 'London Letter: Moral West End,' *Hudson Review*, XIV, no. 1 (Spring 1961), 93–103. Survey.

———. 'The Play of Words,' *Listener* (London), LXVIII (12 July 1962), 55–7.

Dorst, Tankred. 'The End of Playwriting,' *Antioch Review*, XXXI (Summer 1971), 255–65. Advocates 'a more democratic theater, an open theater, in which our lives are truly reflected.'

Douglas, Reid. 'The Failure of English Realism,' *Tulane Drama Review*, VII, no. 2 (Winter 1962), 180–3. 'Certainly in the present movement what purports to be an accurate study is frequently only the trappings of realism raised on a foundation as contrived and commercially astute as any long-run farce.'

'Drama at the B.B.C.,' *Plays and Players* (London), XIII, no. 3 (December 1965), 8–12. Survey.

'Dramatic Horizons,' *Author* (London), LXXXI (Spring 1970), 23–5. On repertory theatres.

Driver, Tom F. 'The Best Are Avant-Garde,' *Christian Century*, LXXVII (31 August 1960), 999–1000.

'Dublin,' *Plays and Players* (London), I, no. 1 (October 1953), 25. Survey.

Duncan, Ronald. 'Write With Both Hands,' *Drama* (London), no. 31 (Winter 1953), 17–20. 'I believe that poets can find their place in the theatre again, if they will learn to discipline their verse to the drama.'

———. 'The Language of Theatre Today,' *Drama* (London), no. 50 (Autumn 1958), 26–7. 'Poetry is not served when it is written at one remove from the spoken word.'

———. 'A Preface to the Sixties,' *London Magazine*, VII (July 1960), 15–19. Mainly on the English Stage Company.

'Eclipse,' *Plays and Players* (London), VIII, no. 3 (December 1960), 20. Editorial on 'the change that has been taking place in the West End theatre over the past few years. Once again it has been proved that playgoers are beginning to appreciate that the play's the thing, and not the stars who happen to be appearing in it.'

Edwards, James. 'Dublin,' *Plays and Players* (London), I, no. 10 (July 1954), 22. Survey.

Egri, Péter. 'Anger and Form,' *Zeitschrift für anglistik und Amerikanistik* (East Berlin), XI (1963), 269–80. Review article.

Elliott, Michael. 'Television Drama: The Medium and the Predicament,' *Encore* (London), IV (March–April 1958), 30–7.

Elsom, John. 'The Future Past,' *London Magazine*, IX (September 1969), 101–8. On the dramatists of the late fifties.

'English Theatre Today,' *International Theatre Annual*, III (1957–8), 140–66. Contributions by Robert Bolt, John Hall, Bernard Kops and Derek Monsey.

'Enter the Second Wave,' *Times Literary Supplement*, no. 3309 (29 July 1965), 653–4.

Esslin, Martin. 'The Theatre of the Absurd,' *Tulane Drama Review*, IV, no. 4 (May 1960), 3–15. Tries to explain why the absurd plays, 'although they have suffered their share of protests and scandals, do arouse interest and are received with laughter and thoughtful respect.'

———. 'Must Contemporary Drama Be Sordid?' *Drama* (London), no. 74 (Autumn 1964), 30–3. '. . . the solution of the problem lies in providing every kind of drama, each at the right time.'

———. 'Drama at the BBC,' *Plays and Players* (London), XIII, no. 5 (February 1966), 65. An interview by the Head of BBC Sound Drama.

———. 'Brecht and the English Theatre,' *Tulane Drama Review*, XI, no. 2 (Winter 1966), 63–70. 'That future historians of English drama will describe the period since 1956 as an era of Brechtian influence is quite possible.'

———. 'The Theater of Cruelty,' *New York Times Magazine*, (6 March 1966), 22–3, 71–4. 'There is much cruelty in the theater today, but there is no movement that could be correctly described as a Theater of Cruelty.'

———. 'Contemporary English Drama and the Mass Media,' *English*, XVIII (Spring 1969), 5–11. In the age of mass media, 'drama no longer is synonymous with live theatre.'

———. 'The Mind as a Stage,' *Theatre Quarterly* (London), I (July–September 1971), 5–11. The Head of BBC Radio Drama analyses the techniques of drama in sound radio.

Evans, Gareth Lloyd. 'National and Provincial,' *Guardian* (London) (15 April 1965), p. 8. On Midland Theatres.

'Fair Exchange,' *Plays and Players* (London), VIII, no. 8 (May 1961), 20. Editorial on exchanges between the West End and the repertory theatres in the provinces.

Fallon, Gabriel. 'Why Is There No Irish Claudel or Mauriac?' *Evening Press* (Dublin) (5 February 1955), p. 5. Irish dramatists do not concern themselves specifically with religious or spiritual themes.

———. 'The Future of the Irish Theatre,' *Studies; An Irish Quarterly Review* (Dublin), XLIV (Spring 1955), 92–100. 'It is possible that we will return to the first principles of Yeats and use them as he intended they should be used—to bring upon the stage the deeper thoughts and emotions of Ireland.'

———. 'Dublin Letter,' *America* (New York), XCVIII, no. 2 (12 October 1957), 46–7. Survey.

———. 'The Abbey Theatre Today,' *Threshold*, III, no. 4 (1959), 24–32. Reflections on the Abbey Theatre during its fifty-six years.

———. 'All This and the Abbey Too,' *Studies; An Irish Quarterly Review* (Dublin), XLVIII, no. 192 (Winter 1959), 434–442. Implies that only an upsurge of Irish dramatic talent will affect the rebirth of Irish theatre.

———. 'The Abbey Theatre Today,' *Iris Hibernia* (Fribourg, Switzerland), IV, no. 3 (1960), 46–54. Survey.

———. 'Dublin's Fourth Theatre Festival,' *Modern Drama*, V, no. 1 (May 1962), 21–6. Survey.

Faughnan, Leslie. 'The Future of the Abbey Theatre: Towards a New Dynamic,' *Studies*, LV (Autumn 1966), 236–46. Calls for 'a re-thinking of its function in our society.'

Fay, Gerard. 'London Panorama,' *Theatre Arts* (New York), XLVI (January 1962), 68–9, 78–9. 'Three directors . . . mark three ways of building fresh theatres today; meanwhile, old theatres fade away.'

———. 'The West-End Theatre in the Television Age,' *Listener* (London), LXX (12 September 1963), 281–3. The radical changes taking place in the London West End theatres are not attributable to the spread of television.

———. 'The Irish Theatre,' *Drama* (London), no. 84 (Spring 1967), 33–5. 'The regular professional theatre barely exists in the Republic of Ireland outside Dublin.'

Ferris, Paul. 'Drama at the BBC,' *Plays and Players* (London), XIII, no. 4 (January 1966), 51. Assessment of 'the Drama Department's work from outside.'

Feynman, Alberta E. 'The Fetal Quality of "Character" in Plays of the Absurd,' *Modern Drama*, IX, no. 1 (May 1966), 18–25. 'As soon as any character takes on real coherence and consistency, the drama ceases to be essentially of the "absurd".'

Findlater, Richard. 'The London Theatre,' *Twentieth Century* (London), CLIII (May 1953), 370–6. Review of the season.

———. 'The Autumnal Stage,' *Twentieth Century*, CLIV (December 1953), 460–8. Review of the season.

———. 'Springtime in Shaftesbury Avenue,' *Twentieth Century*, CLV (April 1954), 364–74. Review of the best plays.

———. 'The Empty Site,' *Drama* (London), no. 46 (Autumn 1957), 23–5. The case for a National Theatre.

———. 'Theatre,' *Twentieth Century* (London), CLXIV (July 1958), 62–6. Britain's urgent need for a national theatre.

———. 'The Shrinking Theatre,' *Twentieth Century*, CLXV

(May 1959), 493–500. Current protection for playhouses is inadequate.

———. 'National Theatre Year,' *Spectator* (London), CCIV (18 March 1960), 385–6. On the 'long, long campaign for a National Theatre.'

———. 'The Way Ahead,' *Twentieth Century* (London), CLXIX (February 1961), 99–105. A general look at the framework of the British theatre today.

———. 'Try Some Tightrope Mathematics,' *Time and Tide* (London), XLIII (19 April 1962), 24–5. 'Not for several years have so many shows been waiting for a theatre.'

———. 'The System,' *World Theatre*,' XIII, nos 1–2 (1964), 9–22. On general organisation of British theatre.

Fitz-Simon, Christopher. 'The Theater in Dublin,' *Modern Drama*, II, no. 3 (December 1959), 289–94. Survey.

'Flops,' *Plays and Players* (London), VII, no. 10 (July 1960), 20. Editorial on who is to blame for the flops in the London theatre.

Ford, John. 'Lunch Line-Up,' *Plays and Players* (London), XVIII, no. 8 (May 1971), 50–1. Survey of lunchtime theatre offerings.

'Forward, Sideways and Back,' *Times Literary Supplement* (London) (10 August 1962), p. 606. 'The past year in the British theatre has been, after the manifold excitements of the previous five, mainly a period of settling and consolidation.'

Fox, R. M. 'Same Program, Fifty Years Later,' *American Mercury*, LXXXI (July 1955), 43–4. The Abbey Theatre on the occasion of its Golden Jubilee.

Frank, Elizabeth. 'The Century Theatre: Playhouse on Wheels,' *Educational Theatre Journal*, VI (March 1954), 25–6. 'It is the aim of the Century Theatre to produce plays which would not normally be shown by touring companies in the district.'

'Free for All,' *The Economist*, CCXXX (15 February 1969), 53. Observations.

Freedman, Morris. 'Violence in the Modern Theater: Notes on the New Senecanism,' *New Mexico Quarterly*, XXXVII (Winter 1968), 386–94. Includes references to Edward Bond and Joe Orton.

Freeman, Les. 'And What the Papers Said,' *Plays and Players* (London), XX, no. 4 (January 1973), 36, 'Exhumes the crits for London's top ten.'

Friel, Brian. 'The Theatre of Hope and Despair,' *Critic*, XXVI (August–September 1967), 13–17. 'I think a Theatre of Hope already exists and will grow stronger.'

———. 'Plays Pleasant and Unpleasant,' *Times Literary Supplement* (London) (17 March 1972), pp. 305–6. On the subjects of Irish Drama then and now.

Fry, Christopher. 'The Contemporary Theatre; A Playwright Speaks,' *Listener* (London) (23 February 1950), pp. 331–2. Deals with the problems of the playwright who uses verse for his working language.

———. 'The Play of Ideas.' *New Statesman and Nation* (London), XXXIX (22 April 1950), 458. Letter to the Editor.

———. 'Poetry in the Theatre,' *Saturday Review* (New York) (21 March 1953), 18–19, 33. Taken from a talk given on the BBC Third Programme.

Garrett, Dan. 'Documentary in the Provinces,' *New Theatre Magazine* (Bristol), XII, no. 3 (1973), 2–4. Attempts to examine the phenomenon of performing documentary plays so widely and frequently in Britain today.

Gassner, John. 'Fabianism and the British Playwrights,' *Theatre Arts* (New York), XXXV (November 1951), 30–1, 92–3. 'The British social play generally displays a moderation as unfortunate in the theatre as it is theoretically admirable in politics.'

———. 'Modern Drama and Society,' *World Theatre*, IV, no. 4 (Winter 1955), 21–34. Social drama has had many modes and styles at its disposal and its interest has been largely the result of individual creation.

———. 'Forms of Modern Drama,' *Comparative Literature*, VII (Spring 1955), 129–43.

Gellert, Roger. 'Scruples of a Reluctant Critic,' *Plays and Players* (London), X, no. 10 (July 1963), 16–17. Maintains that a critic cannot really be impartial.

———. 'Theatricalities,' *New Statesman* (London), LXVII (31 January 1964), 182. On the Theatre of Cruelty.

Gibbs, Ramona. 'Pub Theatre,' *Plays and Players* (London), XIX, no. 12 (September 1972), 54–5. Survey of eight pubs in London 'bringing good theatre to the public.'

Gielgud, Val. 'Some Contemporary Reflections,' *Critical Quarterly*, II (1960), 163–66. Argues against the belief that the present parlous condition of the theatre is due to the popularity of television drama.

———. 'Revolution in the Theatre?' *Drama* (London), no. 77 (Summer 1965), 24–6. '. . . a revolution has been taking place. But neither its process nor its backgrounds have been dramatically picturesque.'

———. 'Death of the Censor,' *Contemporary Review*, CCXIX (July 1971), 10–12.

Gilliatt, Penelope. 'A Consideration of Critics,' *Encore* (London) (November 1959), pp. 21–9. Notes on eight contemporary English drama critics.

———. 'Gale of Shock Rips Across the British Stage,' *Life*, LX (20 May 1966), 88 ff.

Gilman, Richard. 'Theatre: Kinky, Arrogant and Frankly Magnificent,' *Esquire*, LXVI (July 1966), 62–3, 122–4. 'The British theatre, at the very least and in more than one sense, can be said to be ambulatory.'

Glicksberg, Charles Irving. 'The Literature of the Angry Young Men,' *Colorado Quarterly*, VIII (1960), 293–303. '. . . their satire . . . is designed not to revolutionize the English scene but to eliminate those abuses which keep young men of ability cooling their heels on the outside.'

Goacher, Denis. 'Modern Poetic Drama,' *Listener* (London), LII (16 December 1954), 1067–8. '. . . the practical test of a verse play is whether it is actable.'

Gow, Gordan. 'Keeping It Alive,' *Plays and Players* (London), XX, no. 4 (January 1973), 33–5. Looks at the long runs.

———. 'Feeling Famous,' *Plays and Players* (London), XXI, no. 12 (September 1974), 16–20. 'A biographical vogue, albeit on a minor scale, has been evident in the London theatre of late.'

Granger, Derek. 'Themes for New Voices,' *London Magazine*, III, no. 12 (1956), 41–7. Evaluates John Osborne, Colin Wilson, Brendan Behan and Nigel Dennis.

Gray, Ken. 'T. E. on the Abbey,' *Irish Times* (Dublin) (21

July 1966), p. 8. Telefis Eireann's film about the Abbey Theatre.

———. 'Confessions of a TV Playwright,' *Times Literary Supplement* (London) (19 September 1968), pp. 1042–3. An account of early experiences.

Greene, David H. 'Recent English Drama,' *Modern Drama*, V, no. 2 (September 1962), 195–6. Survey.

Gregor, Ian. 'London Letter,' *Hudson Review*, XVII (Summer 1964), 243–9. '. . . six months after the doors were first opened and with half a dozen plays behind them the National Theatre could legitimately claim to have made a decisive impact on the British theatre.'

Griffiths, Gareth. 'New Lines: English Theatre in the Sixties and After,' *Kansas Quarterly*, III, no. 2 (1971), 77–8. Believes that 'the range and numbers of new British playwrights indicate that the English theatre will continue to forage and develop in the decade ahead, and, hopefully, discover its own excellences.'

Grossman, Bernard. 'Need Theatre Breed the Ridiculous?' *Performing Arts Review*, I, no. 2 (1970), 201–6. On nudity and obscenity in the theatre.

Gur'yan, L. 'Aleksei Arbuzov ob angliiskom teatre i kino,' *Novoe vremya*, XXVIII (1969), 19–22. Aleksei Arbuzov discusses the English theatre and cinema.

Guthrie, Tyrone. 'Theatre v Television,' *Plays and Players* (London), XIII, no. 8 (May 1966), 55–6, 70–1. On theatre in the television age.

———. 'Contemporary Theatre,' *Review of English Literature*, VII, no. 4 (October 1966), 9–14. There has been a tendency for the theatre to be completely dominated by the metropolitan cities.

Habicht, Werner. 'Theatre der Sprache: Bemerkungen zu einigen englischen Dramen der Gegenwart,' *Die Neueren Sprachen* (1963), pp. 302–13. On the language of contemporary English drama.

Hackett, Joe. "What Plays Pay,' *New Society*, (3 August 1972), pp. 248–9. '. . . subsidies or no, what makes money in the theatre is likely to remain the same–spectacle, humour and star appeal.

Hahanloser-Ingold, Margrit. 'Spuren Brechts im englischen Theater,' *Neue Zurcher Zeitung* (2 March 1969), p. 53. On the influence of Brecht on English drama.

Hall, John. 'English Theatre Today: II. The Shutters Are Still Up,' *International Theatre Annual*, III (1957–8), 145–50. 'We ought to decentralise the English theatre.'

———. 'British Drama in the Sixties–A Note from London,' *Texas Quarterly*, X (Summer 1967), 15–19. 'Drama in this country is in a glorious mess.'

Hall, W. Glenvil. 'The Labour Party and the Provincial Theatre,' *New Theatre Magazine* (Bristol) (October 1959), pp. 5–7. Welcomes 'the efforts now being able to spread love of the drama in this country.'

Hamilton, Iain. 'Poetry and Poeticality,' *Twentieth Century*, CLI (June 1952), 533–7. Contemporary English drama lacks 'the poetic quality.'

Hamilton, Peter. 'Edinburgh 1962,' *Plays and Players* (London), X, no. 1 (October 1962), 18–21. Survey of Edinburgh Theatre Festival offerings.

———. 'Edinburgh Festival,' *Plays and Players* (London), X, no. 2 (November 1962), 60. Survey.

———. 'Edinburgh 1963–First Two Weeks,' *Plays and*

Players (London), XI, no. 2 (November 1963), 30–1. Survey of Edinburgh Theatre Festival offerings.

Hammond, Jonathan. 'Lunch Line-Up,' *Plays and Players* (London), XVIII, no. 7 (April 1971), 50, no. 10 (July 1971), 50–1, no. 12 (September 1971), 70; XIX, no. 3 (December 1971), 54, no. 4 (January 1972), 51. Survey of lunchtime theatre offerings.

———. 'Fringe,' *Plays and Players* (London), XIX, no. 11 (August 1972), 55, no. 12 (September 1972), 53–4; XX, no. 1 (October 1972), 49–51, no. 2 (November 1972), 62–4, no. 3 (December 1972), 56–8, no. 4 (January 1973), 53–5, no. 5 (February 1973), 46–7, no. 6 (March 1973), 50–2; no. 7 (April 1973), 52–4, no. 8 (May 1973), 52–3; no. 9 (June 1973), 54–5. Survey of lunchtime theatre productions.

———. 'Drama Schools,' *Plays and Players* (London), XX, no. 9 (June 1973), 34–7, no. 10 (July 1973), 34–7; XXI, no. 1 (October 1973), 38–40. Survey.

Hanratty, Jerome. 'Melodrama–Then and Now. Some Possible Lessons from the Nineteenth Century,' *A Review of English Literature*, IV (April 1963), 108–14. '. . . if we study nineteenth century melodrama more seriously we may re-discover qualities in it that can be used to carry a modern consciousness and a modern method of expression.'

'Hard Times,' *Drama* (London), no. 46 (Autumn 1957), 16–17.

Hardie, Margaret. 'Contemporary British Dramatists,' *Cizi jazyky ve skole*, X (1967), 97–104, 145–53.

Hare, Carl. 'Creativity and Commitment in Contemporary British Theatre,' *Humanities Association Bulletin*, XVI, no. 1 (Spring 1965), 21–8. Examines the attitudes of John

Osborne, Arnold Wesker, John Arden and Harold Pinter to commitment and the effect that it has on their plays.

Hawkes, Terence. 'Drama versus the Theatre,' *Listener* (London), LXXVII (1 June 1967), 711–12; (8 June 1967), 734–4. On the present state of the theatre.

Hawkins, W. 'Festive Island '51,' *Theatre Arts* (New York), XXXV (September 1951), 28–9, 92. Survey of the theatrical season during the Festival of Britain.

Hayman, Ronald. 'Like a Woman They Keep Going Back To,' *Drama* (London), XCVIII (Autumn 1970), 57–64. 'Of the playwrights who have emerged in England since 1956, there are none who have completely rejected Naturalism and none . . . who are satisfied with it.'

———. 'The More We Are Together?' *Drama* (London), no. 100 (Spring 1971), 43–52. Pros and cons of ensemble theatre.

———. 'Theatre and Theatres,' *Drama* (London), no. 104 (Spring 1972), 50–9. Examines 'how far the activity of theatre is affected by the buildings available for it and by the prevailing structure of theatrical society.'

———. 'The Royal Court 1956–1972,' *Drama* (London), no. 105 (Summer 1972), 45–53. An account of the English Stage Company.

Hays, H. R. 'Transcending Naturalism,' *Modern Drama*, V, no. 1 (May 1962), 27–36. Examines some of the characteristics of the younger British playwrights.

'Help!' *Plays and Players* (London), VI, no. 10 (July 1959), 20. On the National Theatre.

Henderson, Gordon. 'An Interview with Hilton Edwards and Micheál MacLiammóir,' *Journal of Irish Literature*, II

(May–September 1973), 79–97. On the Dublin Gate Theatre.

Hepple, Peter. 'God Bless America,' *National Review*, XXIV (13 October 1972), 1142. 'American tourists have been drawn by traditional-styled British plays and actors.'

Herbert, Sir Alan. 'Sense in Censorship?' *Listener* (London), LXXV (2 June 1966), 785–6. Argues that as an institution censorship should stay.

Hewes, Henry. 'Broadway Postscript: Dublin,' *Saturday Review* (New York), XL (18 May 1957), 34–5. Dublin begins its first annual theatre festival.

———. 'The September Rising,' *Saturday Review* (New York), XLIII (10 September 1960), 33, 36. Survey of the Dublin International Theatre Festival.

———. 'Looking Both Ways,' *Saturday Review* (New York), XLIII (24 September 1960), 31. Conventional and unconventional subjects side by side.

———. 'Oh What a Lovely Class Struggle,' *Saturday Review* (New York), XLVI (22 June 1963), 33. 'London has come to the end of one of its poorest theatre seasons.'

———. 'Surveying London's Season,' *Saturday Review* (New York), IL (7 May 1966), 101. 11 Musicals, 13 comedy or suspense productions, 2 American plays, 3 revivals and 3 comparatively serious British dramas.

———. 'Theater in England,' *Saturday Review* (New York), LIII (25 July 1970), 20.

———. 'The British Bundle,' *Time*, LIV (11 September 1971), 20, 54. 'The West End can currently boast that it has thirty-four theatres open (Broadway has seventeen), with an overwhelming display of star actors.'

———. 'The London Scene,' *Saturday Review* (New York), LV (8 April 1972), 8–10. Survey.

'Highlights of the London Season,' *Theatre Arts* (New York), XLII (May 1958), 28–31. Survey.

Hobson, Harold. 'State Patronage of the Theater; Britain Stirred by Moral Indignation and Practical Effects of Subsidy Issue,' *Christian Science Monitor Weekly Magazine Section* (7 January 1950), p. 7.

———. 'Poetic Drama Ascendant,' *Christian Science Monitor Weekly Magazine Section* (25 March 1950), p. 4.

———. 'Drama–And Taxes,' *Christian Science Monitor Weekly Magazine Section* (19 August 1950), p. 18.

———. 'The Bag of Gold,' *Plays and Players* (London), X, no. 3 (December 1962), 24–5. On the responsibilities of the drama critic towards the theatre, his readers and himself.

———. See also his regular contributions to *Sunday Times* (London), 1947 to the present.

Hodge, Jane Aiken. 'The English Season,' *Travel and Camera* (August 1969), 41–2, 105. Survey.

Hogan, Robert. 'The Year in Review; 1967. Theatre,' *University Review* (Dublin), V (1968), 103–12. Irish focus.

———. 'Dublin: The Summer Season and the Theatre Festival, 1967,' *Drama Survey*, VI (Spring 1968), 315–23, Survey.

Hoggart, Simon. 'Stage Directions,' *Guardian* (London) (27 January 1969), p. 6. On the Arts Council grants to commercial theatres.

———. 'A Desperate Throw to Save Commercial Theatres,' *Guardian* (London), (26 November 1969), p. 11. On a proposed 'bank' to finance shows and save theatres.

Holder, Owen. 'The Value and Values of Criticism,' *Drama* (London), no. 45 (Summer 1957), 31–3. '. . . the responsibility of cultivating, maintaining and protecting the arts lies not with their practitioners, but with those outside them.'

Holloway, John. 'Tank in the Stalls: Notes on the "School of Anger",' *Hudson Review*, X (Autumn 1957), 424–9. Traces the reaction to the 'angry young men'.

Holmes, Martin. 'Players and Productions,' *Quarterly Review*, CCC (April 1962), 196–205. 'There was quite a varied assortment of theatrical fare in the second half of 1961.

Hope-Wallace, Philip. 'The Play Is Still the Thing,' *United Nations World*, V (6 June 1951), 45–6. 'There is enormous and surely healthy diversity in the London theatre.'

———. 'Theatrical Paradox 1960: Talent Runs to Waste,' *Guardian* (London) (2 January 1960), p. 4. '. . . the chances of the serious new play are extremely poor.'

———. 'Critic As Connoisseur,' *Plays and Players* (London), X, no. 6 (March 1963), 24–5. On the responsibilities of the drama critic.

———. 'Class in the Theatre,' *Twentieth Century*, CLXXIII (Spring 1965), 127–9. The theatre critic of the *Guardian* finds that the class system has been a fertile ground for dramatic exploitation, which has mirrored it without fostering it in the process.

———. 'Twang Goes the Stage,' *Guardian* (London) (18

January 1966), p. 7. 'Our theatre, a beloved invalid, is always ailing. But still seems to cling on.'

———. 'Even the Critics Are Leaving the Theatre,' *Guardian* (London) (29 November 1968), p. 12. 'The whole theatre-going habit seems to have taken a severe knock in the past few years.'

Hornick, Neil. 'All Our Yesterdays–1951,' *Plays and Players* (London) XIV, no. 1 (October 1966), 64–5, 67. Takes a look at the theatre's contribution to this inauguration of a new phase in the brave new world of postwar Britain.

Hughes, Catharine. 'Theatre in Dublin,' *Nation* (New York), CCIX, no. 18 (24 November 1969), 579–81. Survey of the year's Theatre Festival.

———. 'Broadway Hails Britannia,' *America*, CXXIV (16 January 1971), 46–8. '. . . the opening half of the current New York theatre season has been a parade of imported successes from the London stage.'

———. 'Broadway and the British,' *Catholic World*, CCXII (March 1971), 313–15. London and New York productions compared.

———. 'Four Hit Plays–A London Preview,' *America*, CXXVI (8 April 1972), 376–9. Survey.

Hull, Basil E. 'Introducing England,' *Players Magazine*, XXXII (December 1955), 56–7. Survey.

Hunt, Albert. 'Fight the Old Fight,' *New Society* (3 February 1972), pp. 243–4. 'In contrast to Littlewood's Theatre Workshop, the Royal Court has always been an avowedly writer's theatre. The emphasis has been on the text.'

Hunt, Hugh. 'Among the Mortar-Boards,' *Plays and Players* (London), IX, no. 8 (May 1962), 13, 29. Investigates and challenges some confused ideas about drama and the universities.

———. 'A Gown for Cinderella: Drama in the Universities and an Examination of Some of Its Problems,' *Review of English Literature*, VII, no. 4 (October 1966), 15–24.

Igoe, W. J. 'London Letter,' *America*, XCI (14 August 1954), 480–1. Survey.

———. 'London Letter,' *America*, XCV (9 June 1956), 265–6. Survey.

———. 'London Letter,' *America*, XCVI (22 December 1956), 354. Survey.

'In London: End of a Golden Age?' *Time*, XCI (16 February 1968), 76. Observations.

'In the Theatre, 1936–1956; Some First Impressions,' *English*, XI (Summer 1956), 54–6. Reprints of reviews.

'The Irish Theatre: Sick or Sound?' *Aquarius* (Ireland), IV (1971), 17–25. Symposium contributed by Micheál MacLiammóir, Tyrone Guthrie, Eugene McCabe and John D. Stewart.

Isaac, Dan. 'What's Happening with Drama,' *Judaism*, XVI (Fall 1967), 462–74.

Jain, Jasbir. 'Anger in Wilderness: English Drama in Mid-Fifties of the Twentieth Century,' *Rajasthan University Studies in English*, VI (1972), 102–17.

Johns, Eric. 'Cradle for Playwrights,' *Theatre World* (London), LXI, no. 491 (December 1965), 31. On the English Stage Company.

Johnston, Denis. 'What Has Happened to the Irish?' *Theatre*

Arts (New York), XLIII (July 1959), 11–12, 72. 'Today there are probably as many good Irish authors as ever, but the atmosphere of the country is centrifugal rather than the reverse.'

———. 'That's Show Business,' *Theatre Arts* (New York), (February 1960), 82–3, 95. Reflections by an Irish playwright on the production of plays.

Jones, D. A. N. 'Politics in the Theatre,' *Times Literary Supplement* (London) (27 July 1967), pp. 681–2. Illustrations from contemporary British plays.

———. 'British Playwrights,' *Listener*, LXXX; no. 2054 (8 August 1968), 161–3.

———. 'Taking the Fringe Seriously,' *Daily Telegraph Magazine Section* (London) (30 May 1969), pp. 14–17, 19–20. '. . . the fringe, with its unconventional experiments, is rapidly becoming respectable.'

———. 'Silent Censorship in Britain,' *Theatre Quarterly*, I (January–March 1971), 22–8.

Jones, Margaret. 'The Permissive Theatre and Censorship,' *Sydney Morning Herald* (1 May 1969), p. 2; (2 May 1969), p. 2. Looks at some of the arguments for and against the need for restraint–voluntary or involuntary.

Joseph, Stephen. 'No New Playwrights?' *Encore* (London) (June 1957), pp. 42–5. '. . . there is not much experiment.'

'Just Deserts,' *Plays and Players* (London), VII, no. 4 (January 1960), p. 20. Editorial on the lack of encouragement to new dramatists.

Kalem, T. E. 'The View from London,' *Time*, C (18 September 1972), 74–5. Survey.

Kauffmann, Stanley. 'London Theater,' *New Republic*, CLXVII (22 July 1972), 22, 34. 'Broadway is no worse than the West End.'

Kaufmann, R. J. 'On the Supersession of the Modern Classic Style,' *Modern Drama*, II, no. 4 (February 1960), 358–69. '. . . in our own time these traditional usages of the modern drama have undergone and are undergoing a fundamental reworking.'

———. 'On the Newness of the New Drama,' *Tulane Drama Review*, VI, no. 4 (June 1962), 94–106. 'These *new* dramatists grope in the soil of experience for the hidden root of our humanity.'

Kelly, Seamus. 'Where Motley Is Worn,' *Spectator* (London), CXCVI (20 April 1956), 538, 540 '. . . while there is no dearth of acting or writing talent in the Dublin theatre today, there is equally no very adequate economic encouragement for either.'

———. 'Bridgehead Revisited,' *Spectator* (London), CCIV (29 April 1960), 626–8. Survey of drama in Ireland.

Kendall, William. 'The City Fathers and the Theatre,' *Drama* (London), no. 61 (Winter 1962), 36–9. A policy of theatre patronage on the part of local authorities is much needed.

———. 'La conservation des théâtres en Grande Bretagne,' *Theatre Research*, X, no. 2 (1969), 74–81. On saving theatres from demolition.

Kernodle, George R. 'Time-Frightened Playwrights,' *Meanjin*, IX (Winter 1950), 118–26. 'The most terrifying plays show man in the twentieth-century caught in a speeding whirl of time.'

Kerr, Walter. 'Comedy Now,' *Critic*, XXV (April–May 1967),

39–51. Reprinted as a chapter in his *Tragedy and Comedy* (New York: Simon and Schuster, 1967).

———. 'What Can They Do for an Encore?' *New York Times Magazine*, (2 February 1969), pp. 24–30. On the theatre of nudity.

Kilroy, Thomas. 'Groundwork for an Irish Theatre,' *Studies; An Irish Quarterly Review* (Dublin), XLVIII, no. 190 (Summer 1959), 192–8. Suggests that the new Abbey Theatre should try to create a workshop atmosphere where aspiring playwrights would receive an apprenticeship in modern stagecraft and learn by practical experience the requirements of a particular body of actors.

Kingston, Jeremy. 'Are Heads Growing Tinier?' *London Magazine*, VII (July 1960), 19–22. Mainly on the English Stage Company.

Kitchin, Laurence. 'Backwards and Forwards,' *Twentieth Century* (London), CLXIX (February 1961), 165–72. Takes a general view of the drama old and new.

———. 'The Cage and the Scream,' *Listener* (London), LXIX (24 January 1963), 157–9. Considers the plays in which the characters are insulated from society in such a way as to encourage the maximum conflict of attitudes.

———. 'Compressionism–What Is It?' *Plays and Players* (London), X, no. 11 (August 1963), 12–13. 'What it amounts to in drama is a marriage between modern man's prison complex and the proscenium stage's aptitude for boxing actors in.'

———. 'The Theatre of Cruelty,' *Listener* (London), LXX (19 September 1963), 419–21. Many contemporary plays illustrate 'a habit of lingering over the cruelty, of spelling it out.'

———. 'The British Theatre in the Television Age: The Group and the Crowd,' *Listener*, LXXII (10 September 1964), 381–2.

———. 'Realism in the English Mid-Century Drama,' *World Theatre* (UNESCO), XIV, no. 1 (January–February 1965), 17–26. Survey from Robertson to the present.

———. 'Compressionism Today,' *Listener* (London), LXXIII (11 March 1965), 366–8. Considers recent examples of the cheap production budget in the theatre of small casts in a single decor.

Knepler, Henry. 'Translation and Adaptation in the Contemporary Drama,' *Modern Drama*, IV, no. 1 (May 1961), 31–41.

Knight, G. Wilson. 'The Kitchen Sink; On Recent Developments in Drama,' *Encounter*, XXI, no. 6 (December 1963), 48–54. 'In England our Kitchen Sink dramas are, despite their many limitations, probably the strongest single movement in contemporary writing.'

Kops, Bernard. 'English Theatre Today: III. Back Toward the Epic,' *International Theatre Annual*, III (1957–8), 150–60. 'If the theatre does not experiment it will die.'

———. 'The Young Writer and the Theatre,' *Jewish Quarterly*, VIII, no. 3 (1961), 19–20, 22. 'Theatre in England is no longer the precious inner sanctum for the precious few.'

Kott, Jan. 'The Icon and the Absurd,' *Tulane Drama Review*, XIV (Fall 1969), 18–24. 'Each avant-garde dramatist today has developed his own iconographic method.'

Kovalev, I. 'Granitsy "novogo teatra" [The Frontiers of the "New Theatre"],' *Teatr* (Moscow), VIII (1969), 164–8.

Kretzmer, Herbert. 'You Can't Help the Pain,' *Plays and Players* (London), X, no. 12 (September 1963), 14–15. Maintains that a critic must not flinch from causing pain.

La Barre, H. 'Great Theatres of the World–Abbey: Dublin,' *Cosmopolitan* (New York), XCLVII (November 1959), 68–9. Describes the Abbey as 'Ireland's National Theatre showcase for Irish playwrights.'

Lambert, J. W. 'Plays in Performance,' *Drama* (London), no. 31 (Winter 1954), 14–18. 'Of the dozen or so new plays . . . two have attempted to be anything out of the ordinary.'

———. 'The London Theatre Season,' *International Theatre Annual*, I (1955–6), 36–61. Survey.

———. 'The London Theatre,' *International Theatre Annual*, II (1956–7), 11–38. Survey.

———. 'London Theatre,' *International Theatre Annual*, III (1957–8), 11–32. Survey.

———. 'The Season's Work: London,' *International Theatre Annual*, IV (1958–9), 14–51. Survey.

———. 'Mood of the Month-VIII,' *London Magazine*, VI (March 1959), 42–7. Responsibility of the loss of the magic of the theatre 'lies with audiences, dramatists and performers alike.'

———. 'Exit Censor,' *Sunday Times* (London) (22 September 1968), p. 12. On Theatres Act 1968.

Landstone, Charles. 'From John Osborne to Shelagh Delaney,' *World Theatre*, VIII, no. 3 (Autumn 1959), 203–16. Survey.

———. 'Town and Gown: The British Theatre in the

Television Age,' *Listener*, LXXII (2 July 1964), 13–15. The importance of provincial theatres in 'keeping the taste for theatre alive among the local population, while providing a vitally important training ground for the artists, who will later find their way to . . . the West End.'

Lee, Jennie. 'Hands Off the Theatres,' *Sunday Times* (London) (7 February 1971), p. 23. The former Arts Minister explains why Lord Eccles's censorship proposals must be rejected.

Lerman, Leo. 'The English Look,' *Mademoiselle* (New York), LVI (April 1963), 142–5. In entertainment, 'there is a burgeoning of Britishers.'

Levidov, I. 'V teatr prixodit novyj: Zametki o molodyx dramaturgax Anglii [Comments on the young dramatists of England],' *Inostrannaja literatura*, VIII, no. 1 (1962), 201–8.

Levin, Bernard. 'Critic As Journalist,' *Plays and Players* (London), X, no. 7 (April 1963), 14–15. On the responsibilities of the drama critic.

Lewis, Peter. 'Is This What We Got Rid of the Lord Chamberlain for?' *Nova*, (February 1969), 62–5. The removal of censorship so far shows little promise of advancing the art of drama.

'The Lights of London,' *Time*, LXXXIV (9 October 1964), 42. Observations.

Liisberg, Henrik Bering. 'Den moderne engelske dramatik,' *Tvaersnit* (Copenhagen) (1965), pp. 80–110. Deals with John Osborne, Arnold Wesker, John Arden, Harold Pinter, Alun Owen, Henry Livings and Ann Jellicoe.

Linklater, Eric. 'The Language of the Theatre Today,' *Drama* (London), no. 50 (Autumn 1958), 25–6. Reprinted from the appendix to his play *Breakspear in Gascony* (London: Macmillan, 1958). It is difficult to write a great drama in our contemporary idiom.

Lipsius, Frank. 'Edinburgh 72,' *Plays and Players* (London), XX, no. 2 (November 1972), 54. Survey of Edinburgh Festival drama offerings.

Littlewood, John. 'Plays for the People,' *World Theatre*, VIII (Winter 1959–60), 283–90. By employing 'contemporary and vital material,' the theatre can realise its social purpose.

Littlewood, S. R. 'Towards the National Theatre,' *English*, IX, no. 48 (1952), 287–9.

Lodge, David. 'Look Back in Disappointment: A London Theatre Report,' *Critic*, XXV (February–March 1967), 62–5. Survey.

'The London Stage, I–The Managements: The Plight of the West End Theatre,' *The Times* (London) (26 February 1965), p. 16.

'The London Stage, II–The Writer: West End Still the Dramatist's Main Platform,' *The Times* (London) (3 March 1965), p. 15.

'The London Stage, III–Directors and Actors: Self-Indulgence or Security for an Essential Individualist?' *The Times* (London) (17 March 1965), p. 15.

'The London Stage: Exit the Censor,' *Time*, XCII (11 October 1968), 76.

'London Stage: Fossils and Ferment,' *Time*, XCII (9 August 1968), 64ff.

'London's the Place for Playgoing,' *Sunset*, CXXXIV

(February 1965), 34–5. Comparison between playgoing in London and New York.

Loney, Glenn M. 'Theatre of the Absurd: It Is Only a Fad,' *Theatre Arts* (New York), XLVI (November 1962), 20, 22, 24, 66–8. Argues that the Theatre of the Absurd 'is very much a function of our era, though it derives many of its techniques and much of its nihilism from the theatre and philosophy of earlier periods.'

———. 'London's Subsidized Theatres,' *Quarterly Journal of Speech*, LII, no. 1 (February 1966), 63–9. The National Theatre, the Royal Shakespeare, the Mermaid, and the English Stage Society since 1950.

Lothian, Andrew. 'Edinburgh Festival,' *Plays and Players* (London), XVII, no. 1 (October 1969), 50–1. Survey of drama offerings.

Lucas, Walter. 'Stage Sixty–Interdrama 65,' *Drama* (London), no. 78 (Autumn 1965), 32–5. Survey of the new Stage Sixty company's productions and of Interdrama 65 Festival.

———. 'More Than a Beginning,' *Drama* (London), no. 81 (Summer 1966), 27–9. 'The institution of what we hope will be known as the British Theatre Centre in Fitzroy Square marks a leap forward.'

———. 'Home and Abroad,' *Drama* (London), no. 97 (Summer 1970), 64–7. Survey.

MacCall, Ewan. 'Grass Roots of Theatre Workshop,' *Theatre Quarterly* (London), III (January–March 1973), 58–68. Records the facts about the early years of Joan Littlewood's Theatre Workshop.

McCormick, Kevin. 'The Spirit of 67 Lives On,' *Plays and*

Players (London), XIX, no. 11 (August 1972), 30–2. On the theatre of peace, love and innocence.

McDonald, Daniel. 'Science, Literature, and Absurdity,' *South Atlantic Quarterly*, LXVI (Winter 1967), 42–9. 'Many of the new dramas depict a Wonderland which . . . reflect the scientific complexity of their day.'

Macgowan, Kenneth. 'The Educational Theatre for Tomorrow,' *Educational Theatre Journal*, IX, no. 2 (May 1957), 85–95. Examines the present objectives to see how they can be 'wisely changed and amplified.'

McHugh, Roger. 'Drama in Ireland Today,' *Iris Hibernia* (Fribourg, Switzerland), IV, no. 3 (1960), 40–2. 'I think that Ireland is in for a second wave of good dramatic writing.'

McLaughlin, John J. 'The Future of Farce,' *Journal of Popular Culture*, III (1970), 729–35. 'Farce has virtually taken over television.'

MacOwan, Michael. 'This Age of Discovery,' *Plays and Players* (London), I, no. 1 (October 1953), 10. 'The dramatist of today is more often asking a question than telling us the answer.'

MacWilliam, Bourke. 'Dublin,' *Plays and Players* (London), II, no. 6 (March 1955), 26, no. 7 (April 1955), 26, no. 8 (May 1955), 26, no. 9 (June 1955), 23, no. 10 (July 1955), 23, no. 11 (August 1955), 23; III, no. 1 (October 1955), 28, no. 2 (November 1955), 23. Survey.

———. 'Ireland,' *Plays and Players* (London), III, no. 3 (December 1955), 26, no. 5 (February 1956), 17, no. 7 (April 1956), 16, no. 11 (August 1956), 32. Survey.

Mander, Gertrud. 'Die jungen englischen Dramatiker,' *Neue deutsche Hefte*, LXXXIII (1961), 104–20. The young English dramatists.

Mannes, Marya. 'A Seat in the Stalls,' *Reporter*, XIII (20 October 1955), 42–3. Survey of theatre productions.

———. 'Just Looking, Thanks,' *Reporter*, XXIII (13 October 1960), 48–9. Survey of theatre productions.

Manvell, Roger. 'Revolution in the British Theatre,' *Humanist*, LXXXV (March 1970), 77–9. Review article.

———. 'Humanist Theatre,' *Humanist*, LXXXVII (January 1972), 27–8. On the recent productions of the Royal Court Theatre.

Marcus, Frank. '10 Years On,' *Plays and Players* (London), XX, no. 7 (April 1973), 18–22. Looks back on a decade of World Theatre in London.

——— 'Why Save Our Theatres?' *Plays and Players*, XX, no. 11 (August 1973), 14–15.

Marowitz, Charles. 'New Wave in a Dead Sea,' *X: A Quarterly Review*, I (1960), 270–7. The theatre of social realism in London: John Osborne, Samuel Beckett, Brendan Behan, Harold Pinter and N. F. Simpson.

———. 'Anger and the Absurd,' *Plays and Players* (London), IX, no. 11 (August 1962), 57. Review article.

———. 'What Happened to *Encore*,' *Plays and Players* (London), XIII, no. 3 (December 1965), 13. Explains the demise of the publication.

———. 'State of Play,' *Tulane Drama Review*, XI, no. 2 (Winter 1966), 203–6. 'The best decade in the English theatre has been a real gasser . . . but it's only brought England to a new starting point and not . . . to a finish-line.'

Marshall, Norman. 'Avantgarde or Rearguard?' *London*

Magazine, VII (July 1960), 22–5. '. . . in England we persist in ignoring what has been going on for many years in the theatres of other countries.'

———. 'Banned!' *Drama* (London), no. 85 (Summer 1967), 30–3. Review article on censorship.

Martin, Troy Kennedy. 'Nats Go Home,' *Encore* (London), XI (March–April 1964), 21–33. Observations on television drama.

Masters, Anthony. 'Soho Poly Season,' *Plays and Players* (London), XXI, no. 3 (December 1973), 59. Survey of the lunchtime theatre.

Mathieson, Andrew. 'The Dark East,' *Drama* (London), no. 93 (Summer 1969), 45–9. Survey of Stratford East productions from 1884 to the present.

Matthews, Harold. 'Dublin Festival 1965,' *Theatre World* (London), LXI, no. 490 (November 1965), 17–19, 23. Survey.

May, Frederick. 'Drama in the Universities,' *Universities Quarterly*, (February 1951), 155–61. Should drama be taught in the universities?

———. 'Practical Drama [in the Universities],' *Universities Quarterly*, (February 1956), 166–71.

Mayes, Herbert R. 'London Letter: Two on the Isle,' *Saturday Review* (New York), LIV (5 June 1971), 6–7. London and New York prices.

Mayne, Rutherford. 'The Ulster Literary Theatre,' *Dublin Magazine*, XXXI (April–June 1955), 15–21. This theatre, which celebrated its Golden Jubilee in 1954, has a tradition of fine actors and unique plays, with 1904–9 being a particular rich period in its history.

Meisel, Martin. 'Recent Drama Criticism,' *Contemporary Literature*, X (Summer 1969), 396–415. Review article.

Mercier, Vivian. 'The Dublin Tradition,' *New Republic* (New York), CXXXV, no. 6 (6 August 1956), 21–2. Argues that in Dublin 'a healthy theatre is living off its traditions.'

Merson, John. 'Edinburgh 1965,' *Plays and Players* (London), XIII, no. 2 (November 1965), 22. Survey of Edinburgh Theatre Festival.

Michel, Laurence. 'The Possibility of a Christian Tragedy,' *Thought*, XXXI (1956), 403–28. '. . . nothing in literature has yet come forth which is both Christian and tragedy at the same time.'

Miller, Jonathan. 'Censorship,' *Guardian* (London) (16 October 1967), p. 6.

Miller, Liam. 'Eden and After: The Irish Theatre 1945–1966,' *Studies*, LV (Autumn 1966), 231–5. Surveys the Irish Theatre since the end of World War II and concludes that 'however one looks at the situation today, it is on the National Theatre that our hopes for the future of the theatre in Ireland must be based.'

Milne, Tom. 'The Hidden Face of Violence,' *Encore* (London), VII, no. 1 (1960), 14–20. Reprinted in *Modern British Dramatists*, ed. John Russell Brown (Englewood Cliffs, New Jersey: Prentice–Hall, 1968), pp. 38–46. On John Whiting, Harold Pinter and John Arden.

Mitchell, James. 'Theatres for the People,' *Drama* (London), no. 79 (Winter 1965), 28–30. On the spread of civic theatres in the sixties.

'The Modern Theater, or, The World as a Metaphor of Dread,' *Time* (8 July 1966), pp. 34–5. 'What these modern playwrights aim for is not to convey actions, messages or answers but states of being and feeling.'

'Money Behind the Scenes,' *The Economist*, CXCVI (6 August 1960), 540–1. 'The London theatre, at least, is alive artistically and a draw financially.'

Monsey, Derek. 'English Theatre Today: IV. The Criminal Intellectual,' *International Theatre Annual*, III (1957–8), 160–6. 'The English theatre, particularly the English drama, is today writhing in a strait-jacket imposed upon it by the intellectuals.'

Moore, Mavor. 'The Decline of Words in Drama,' *Canadian Literature*, XLVI (1970), 11–18. Suggests 'the various influences which seem—at an astonishing pace—to be shaping the theatre and the lyric theatre of today and tomorrow.'

Morgan, Edwin. 'The Novel and the Drama,' *English* (London), XVI (1967), 227–9. On Scottish writing today.

Morley, Sheridan. 'To Save or Not To Save,' *Plays and Players* (London), XIX, no. 12 (September 1972), 33. On the demolition of theatres.

Mortimer, John. 'End or Change Stage Censorship,' *Plays and Players* (London), IX, no. 12 (September 1962), 22. Reflections.

———. 'After the Chamberlain,' *Author* (London), LXXXI (Summer 1970), 70–1. The Theatres Act of 1968 has elevated the status of dramatists 'to the most carefully protected of all public performers.'

Moseley, Virginia. 'A Week in Dublin,' *Modern Drama*, IV, no. 2 (September 1961), 164–71. Survey and panel discussion.

Mulrine, Stephen. 'Fringe Benefits,' *Plays and Players* (London), XXII, no. 1 (October 1974), 22–3. Survey of the year's fringe theatre.

Murray, Geoffrey. 'Church and Stage; A Report from London,' *Christian Century*, LXXVII (3 February 1960), 137–8. On religious drama.

'National Need,' *Plays and Players* (London), V, 23 (December 1957), 20. On the need for a National Theatre.

'The National Theatre,' *Plays and Players* (London), I, no. 1 (October 1953), 3. Editorial.

'National Theatre–Now or Never!' *Plays and Players* (London), VIII, no. 8 (May 1961), 5. The case for a National Theatre as presented by the Joint Council of the National Theatre to the Chancellor of the Exchequer.

'New Abbey Theatre by End of 1960,' *Irish Times* (Dublin (22 October 1958), pp. 1, 7. Description of the sketch plans for the new building.

'A New English Theatre?' *London Magazine*, VII (July 1960), 11–39. Contributions by John Arden, Ronald Duncan, Jeremy Kingston, Norman Marshall, Alan Pryce-Jones, Robert Shaw, John Whiting and Casper Wrede.

'New Plays,' *Plays and Players* (London), I, no. 4 (January 1954), 3. Editorial.

'New Things Happening,' *Times Literary Supplement* (London) (27 October 1961), p. 775. '. . . there is a splinter-group at work . . . decreasing the importance of what is said and increasing the importance of what happens . . . in the building-up of thin plays' final meaning.'

'New Voices,' *Plays and Players* (London), VI, no. 1 (October

1958), 20 'The daring and ambitious English Stage Company . . . set out to revive the dying British drama.'

Nichols, Dorothy. 'Poets As Playwrights,' *Southern Review*, IV (January 1968), 264–70. Review article.

Nightingale, Benedict. 'Theatrical Pressure,' *Guardian* (London) (19 May 1964), p. 8. On the threat of the big subsidised companies.

———. 'Why Preserve Shaftesbury Avenue?' *New Statesman* (London) (28 July 1972), pp. 136–7. Would the loss of the London theatres threatened by redevelopment really matter?

'No Medals,' *Plays and Players* (London), VIII, no. 5 (February 1961), 20. Editorial denouncing the fact that no tribute has been paid to dramatists in the New Year Honours List.

'Not Verse for Plays Now, Only Prose,' *The Times* (London) (21 December 1961), p. 3.

O'Callaghan, John. 'Disabling Vanity,' *Guardian* (London) (29 June 1963), p. 5. 'The professional theatre and our university (and similar) companies are complementrary and contributory the one to the other.'

———. 'The British Theatre in the Television Age: Come-Back in the North-West?' *Listener* (London), LXXI (9 January 1964), 51–3. 'The future for the commercial theatre in the north-west looks grim.'

O'Connor, Ulick. 'Dublin's Dilemma,' *Theatre Arts* (New York), XL, No. 7 (July 1956), 64–5, 96. Comparison between the Irish theatre now and 'the golden years of the Abbey.'

O'Donnell, Donat. 'The Abbey: Phoenix Infrequent,'

Commonweal (New York), LVII (30 January 1953), 423–4. 'Social calm, literary indolence and dialect conventions' are some of the reasons 'why the flame of the Abbey burns low just now.'

Okumura, Mifune. 'Igirisu Engeki (1956–69) to Shigeki,' *Eigo Seinen* [The Rising Generation] (Tokyo), CXVI (1970), 66–8. Poetic drama in contemporary English theatre.

Oliver, Cordelia. 'Edinburgh,' *Plays and Players* (London), XIX, no. 1 (October 1971), 54–5, 77. Survey of Edinburgh Festival drama offerings.

———. 'Edinburgh,' *Plays and Players* (London), XX, no. 1 (October 1972), 56, no. 2 (November 1972), 51–4. Survey of Edinburgh Festival drama offerings.

———. 'Edinburgh,' *Plays and Players* (London), XXI, no. 1 (October 1973), 64–5, no. 2 (November 1973), 61–2. Survey of Edinburgh Festival drama offerings.

———. 'Festival Time: Edinburgh; Official Offerings,' *Plays and Players* (London), XXII, no. 1 (October 1974), 20–2. Survey.

Oliver, William I. 'After Absurdity,' *Educational Theatre Journal*, XVII, no. 3 (October 1965), 196–205. Absurdity 'might very well prove the force that will intelligently reawaken our drama of social action.'

———. 'Theatre Aesthetics in Crisis,' *Educational Theatre Journal*, XXI (March 1969), 17–27. 'One of the basic causes of our confusion is the simple truth that we have exhausted our enthusiasm for our "ancestral" realism and are prone to attack the form and view of realism itself without ever having understood their function or their communicative possibilities.'

O'Mahony, T. P. 'Theatre in Ireland,' *Eire-Ireland*, IV (Summer 1969), 93–100. Comparison between the Irish theatre then and now.

O'Malley, Mary. 'Theatre in Belfast,' *Iris Hibernia* (Fribourg, Switzerland), IV, no. 3 (1960), 50–7. Survey of theatrical activities in Belfast past and present.

———. 'Irish Theater Letter,' *Massachusetts Review*, VI, (1965), 181–6. On the Lyric Players Theatre, Belfast.

'On Stage Verse,' *Times Literary Supplement* (London) (5 July 1963), p. 493. Review article.

'1,500 New Actors Each Year Compete for 400–500 Jobs,' *The Times* (London) (2 March 1964), p. 14.

Osborn, Tom. 'Le Royal Court Théâtre fait peau neuve,' *Les Lettres Nouvelles*, (February 1964), 137–42.

Page, Malcolm. 'Experimental Theatre in London: A Guide to the "Off-West End",' *Kansas Quarterly*, III, no. 2 (1971), 118–26. 'Since 1967 London has developed an "Off Shaftesbury-Avenue", low-budget, experimental theatre, complementing the thirty-five long-established West End playhouses.'

———. 'Television Drama in Britain,' *Quarterly Journal of Speech*, LVII (1971), 214–20. Discusses the television play as a distinct form of drama.

Page, Sean. 'The Abbey Theatre,' *Dublin Magazine*, V, nos 3–4 (Autumn–Winter 1966), 6–14. Examines the Abbey as a national theatre.

Palfy, Istvan. 'Modern English Drama Through Hungarian Eyes,' *Hungarian Studies in English* (L. Kossuth University, Debrecen), V (December 1971), 137–49. How English drama is received by Hungarian critics and audiences.

———. 'Az abszurdumtol az eroszakig,' *Fillogiai Kozlony*, XVII (1971), 157–64. On contemporary drama.

Panter-Downes, Mollie. 'Letter from London,' *New Yorker*, XLIX (25 May 1963), 148–52. Survey.

———. 'Letter from London,' *New Yorker*, XLIX (21 November 1964), 200–1. Survey.

Parker, Gerald. 'The Modern Theatre as Autonomous Vehicle,' *Modern Drama*, XVI (December 1973), 373–91. The drama which is freed from the precedency of articulate poetry seems 'to posit as the ideal audience either the mindlessly frenzied or the narcotically numbed.'

Parker, R. B. 'The Theory and Theatre of the Absurd,' *Queen's Quarterly*, LXXIII, no. 3 (Autumn 1966), 421–41.

Parry, John. 'Morality and the New Drama,' *Contemporary Review*, CCII (November 1962), 252–6. The new dramatists 'tend to search for a reality underneath the received view of people and their supposed motives.'

Parsons, Philip. 'Dialogue on Popular Theatre,' *Westerly*, no. 1 (1961), 14–18. '. . . today . . . no serious, thoughtful, provocative young dramatist stands much chance in the big-time commercial theatre of the West End.'

Paul, Leslie. 'The Angry Young Men Revisited,' *Kenyon Review*, XXVII, no. 2 (1965), 344–52. An evaluation of the accomplishments of the angry young men.

Pearson, Kenneth. 'Stages for the People,' *Sunday Times* (London) (17 October 1971), p. 35. Across the country new theatres are being built.

Peinert, Dietrich. 'Interpretationshilfen zum neueren englischen und amerikanischen Drama,' *Literatur in*

Wissenschaft und Unterricht (Kiel), IV (1971), 52–65. Interpretations to some modern British plays.

Perrick, Eve. 'So You Think That's Funny?' *Plays and Players* (London), XX, no. 3 (December 1972), 31. Looks at new British comedies 'through pained transatlantic eyes.'

Peschmann, Hermann. 'The Nonconformists: Angry Young Men, "Lucky Jims", and "Outsiders",' *English*, XII (Spring 1960), 12–16. In England at the present various labels are attached to a group who have primarily one thing in common: nonconformity. They are 'in rebellion against certain aspects of their milieu', and they contribute a needed 'vitality' to letters.

Pettet, Edwin Burr. 'Report on the Irish Theatre,' *Educational Theatre Journal*, VIII (May 1956), 109–14. Survey.

Playfair, Giles. 'Theatre of Cowardice,' *New Society* (7 January 1965), p. 22. On the importance of theatres outside the West End.

———. 'Phoney War,' *Spectator* (London) (17 June 1966), p. 754. The theatre 'cannot live, or at least progress, without the critics.'

'Plays and People,' *Drama* (London), no. 83 (Winter 1966), 18–19. Comments on a variety of topics.

'Plays and Plebeians,' *Drama* (London), no. 47 (Winter 1957), 17. 'There is a group in the theatre which implies . . . that the only plays now needed are plebeian plays.'

'Plays in Performance,' *Drama* (London). A quarterly review in every issue.

Popkin, Henry. 'Import Trade,' *World Theatre* (UNESCO),

XV (November–December 1966), 474–8. On the 'influx of British theatre.'

Popovici-Teodoreanu, Liliana. 'Teatrul absurdului în varianta engleză [The Theatre of the Absurd in its English Variant],' *Studii de literatură universală*, X (1967), 109–26.

Porterfield, Christopher. 'The Player's the Thing,' *Time*, XCVI (14 September 1970), 46. Survey.

———. 'Pick of the London Season,' *Time*, XCVIII (30 August 1971), 44–5. Survey.

Price, Martin. 'The London Season,' *Modern Drama*, I, no. 1 (May 1958), 53–9. Survey.

Priestly, J. B. 'Censor and Stage,' *New Statesman* (London) (17 December 1965), p. 967. 'We may need some form of censorship but it should represent not the Establishment but theatrical experience and some knowledge of public taste and feeling.'

'The Profitable Stage,' *The Economist*, CCXLI (4 December 1971), 30–1.

Pryce-Jones, Alan. 'Is a National Theatre Necessary?' *London Magazine*, VII (July 1960), 25–30.

———. 'The British National Theatre,' *Theatre Arts* (New York), XLVII (November 1963), 20–1, 78–9. '. . . a fact after a century of frustration.'

Pye, Michael. 'Drama in the Universities,' *Plays and Players* (London), XII, no. 11 (August 1965), 10–12. Survey.

Randall, Jeremy. 'Fresh Sap for the Withered Tree,' *Tulane Drama Review*, XI, 2 (Winter 1966), 132–7. On repertories.

Rattigan, Terence. 'Concerning the Play of Ideas,' *New Statesman and Nation* (London), XXXIX (4 March 1950), 241–2. 'I believe that the best plays are about people and not about things.' See reply by G. Lewis (11 March 1950), 274; and rejoinder (13 May 1950), 545–6.

'The Reaction Against Realism,' *Times Literary Supplement* (London) (30 June 1961), p. 400. Review article on Harold Pinter, John Osborne, Shelagh Delaney, John Arden and Alun Owen.

'The Realistic Mode,' *Times Literary Supplement* (London) (20 January 1961), p. 42. Review article.

'Rebels with a Cause,' *Plays and Players* (London), III, no. 11 (August 1956), 3. On the new dramatists who have in common 'a determination to bring our drama back to grips with the harsh realities of life.'

Rebora, Piero. 'Teatro inglese contemporaneo,' *Nuova Antologia*, CDLXVI (February 1956), 281–90. Survey.

'Red Ladder Now,' *New Theatre Magazine* (Bristol), XII, no. 3 (1973), 23–9. An account of the Red Ladder Theatre, London.

Reid, Alec. 'Dublin's Abbey Theatre Today,' *Drama Survey*, III, no. 4 (Fall 1964), 507–19. A brief history of the Abbey Theatre plus some observations on its organisation today and its plans for the future.

'Rep in the Balance,' *Plays and Players* (London), XII, no. 11 (September 1965), 8–14, 46–8. Views on the state of the repertory theatre.

'Repertoire contemporain en Angleterre,' *Cahiers de la Compagnie Madeleine Renaud-Jean Louis Barrault*, LV

(1966), 14–23. Survey of repertory theatre productions in London 1956–66.

Repertory,' *Plays and Players* (London), V, no. 11 (August 1958), 22. Editorial on the fiftieth anniversary of repertory theatres in England.

'Repertory Needs,' *Plays and Players* (London), IX, no. 6 (March 1962), 7. Editorial on the repertory movement outside London.

'Report from an Angel,' *The Economist*, CCXV (17 April 1965), 306–7. On West End Theatre economics.

'Reverse English,' *Theatre Arts* (New York), XL (October 1956), 16. Nudity in the English theatre.

Richler, Mordecai. 'Making Out in the Television Drama Game,' *Twentieth Century* (London), CLXV (March 1959), 235–45. 'Indeed, it seems to me that there's no such thing today as serious television drama.'

Roberts, Peter. 'Dublin Festival,' *Plays and Players* (London), X, no. 2 (November 1962), 61–3. Survey.

———. 'Edinburgh 1963–Third Week,' *Plays and Players* (London), XI, no. 2 (November 1963), 32–3. Survey of Edinburgh Theatre Festival.

———. 'Mixed Blessings,' *Plays and Players* (London), XII, no. 2 (November 1964), 8–9. Survey of the 1964 Dublin Theatre Festival.

———. 'Dublin 1965,' *Plays and Players* (London), XIII, no. 3 (December 1965), 19–22. Survey of Dublin Theatre Festival.

———. 'Dublin Theatre Festival,' *Plays and Players* (London), XIV, no. 2 (November 1966), 56–9, 67. Survey.

———. 'Operation Survival,' *Plays and Players* (London), XV, no. 3 (December 1967), 46–7, 50. Survey of the 1967 Dublin Theatre Festival.

———. 'Dublin,' *Plays and Players* (London), XVI, no. 3 (December 1968), 64–6. Survey of the 1968 Dublin Theatre Festival.

———. 'Dublin,' *Plays and Players* (London), XVIII, no. 8 (May 1971), 53–5. Survey of the 1971 Dublin Theatre Festival.

Robinson, Robert. 'The Lively Art,' *New Statesman* (London), LVI (29 November 1958), 763. Review article.

Rodger, Ian. 'The Moron As Hero,' *Drama* (London), no. 59 (Winter 1960), 36–9. 'The theatre is currently being visited by a school of writing which has chosen the moron as hero.'

Rogoff, Gordon. 'Richard's Himself Again: Journey to an Actors' Theatre,' *Tulane Drama Review*, XI, no. 2 (Winter 1966), 29–40.

Roose-Evans, James. 'How Should the Theatre Grow?' *Drama* (London), no. 97 (Summer 1970), 57–61. '. . . for the theatre to survive, subsidizing is essential.'

Rosenberg, James. 'Looking for the Third World: Theatre Report from England,' *Arts in Society*, VI (1969), 438–44. Survey of theatre productions.

Rosenfield, Judith. 'Belfast,' *Plays and Players* (London), XVI, no. 6 (March 1969), 62–3. Survey.

Rosenfield, Ray. 'Belfast,' *Plays and Players* (London), I, no. 12 (September 1954), 26; II, no. 1 (October 1954), 26, no. 3 (December 1954), 26, no. 4 (January 1955), 26, no. 8 (May 1955), 26, no. 9 (June 1955), 23; III, no. 4 (January 1956), 30, no. 8 (May 1956), 33, no. 11 (August

1956), 33, no. 12 (September 1956), 33; IV, no. 1 (October 1956), 33, no. 2 (November 1956), 32, no. 4 (January 1957), 30, no. 5 (February 1957), 33, no. 6 (March 1957), 32, no. 9 (June 1957), 32, no. 10 (July 1957), 32; V, no. 2 (November 1957), 32, no. 4 (January 1958), 32, no. 6 (March 1958), 33, no. 9 (June 1958), 32, no. 12 (September 1958), 32; VI, no. 1 (October 1958), 33, no. 2 (November 1958), 32, no. 3 (December 1958), 32, no. 5 (February 1959), 32, no. 6 (March 1959), 33, no. 7 (April 1959), 32 no. 9 (June 1959), 32, no. 10 (July 1959), 33, no. 11 (August 1959), 32; VII, no. 1 (October 1959), 33, no. 3 (December 1959), 31–2, no. 5 (February 1960), 33, no. 6 (March 1960), 32, no. 7 (April 1960), 31, no. 11 (August 1960), 33, no. 12 (September 1960), 31–2; VIII, no. 2 (November 1960), 31, no. 5 (February 1961), 33, no. 6 (March 1961), 33, no. 7 (April 1961), 32, no. 9 (June 1961), 36, no. 10 (July 1961), 37, no. 11 (August 1961), 34, no. 12 (September 1961), 34–5; IX, no. 3 (December 1961), 35, no. 4 (January 1961), 28. Survey.

Rosselli, John. 'Mood of the Month–V,' *London Magazine*, V (September 1958), 39–44. The fact that the device of turning legitimate theatres into 'clubs' to present certain plays is working satisfactorily, indicates that there is little being said of overwhelming importance.

———. 'The Importance of Writing Good Plays,' *Reporter*, XXXVI (18 May 1967), 44–9. The public 'has had enough of unpleasant plays,' and prefers revivals, particularly of Wilde's plays and those of the 1920's.

Roud, Richard. 'The Theatre on Trial,' *Encounter*, XI (July 1958), 27–32. Cf. Jens Arup and George Richards, ibid. (September 1958), 74–6 and Stephen Joseph (October 1958), 70–1. Three drama critics–T.C. Worsley, Kenneth Tynan and Philip Hope-Wallace–and their verdicts and what they said about the role and purposes of theatre criticism.

Roy, Claude. 'Lettres anglaises sur le théâtre,' *Nouvelle revue française* (March 1965), 515–26. Reflections on the English theatre.

Rushe, Desmond. 'When the Wind Blows,' *Éire-Ireland*, V, no. 4 (1970), 84–7. Abbey Theatre productions 1969–70.

Russell, John W. 'A Tory and the Provincial Drama,' *New Theatre Magazine* (Bristol) (January 1960), pp. 11–14. On the policy of the Conservative government towards the Theatre.

Ryan, Stephen P. 'Theatre in Dublin,' *America* (New York), XCII (30 October 1954), 128–9. Survey.

———. 'London, 1955,' *America* (New York), XCIII (9 July 1955), 372–4. On 'the less well-known London world of the theatre–less well-known, that is, than the commercial theatre of the West End'.

———. 'Crisis in Irish Letters; Literary Life in Dublin,' *Commonweal* (New York), LXXI, no. 12 (18 December 1959), 347–9. 'The present crop of dramatists includes men of more than average talent . . . but simply not endowed with the touch of genius necessary for enduring fame in the theater.'

———. 'The London Stage; Rave Reviews for the Season Past, One of the Most Stimulating in Years,' *America* (New York), CVII (27 October 1962), 956–8.

Ryapolova, V. 'Posle gneva–ustalost': Angliiskaya dramaturgiya na poroge 70-kh [After the Anger–Weariness: English Dramaturgy at the Threshold of the Seventies],' *Teater* (Moscow), III (1970), 131–6.

Saint-Denis, Michel. 'The English Theatre in Gaelic Eyes,'

Texas Quarterly, IV, no. 3 (Autumn 1961), 26–45. Reflections on the English theatre by a French director.

St John-Stevas, Norman. 'The Censor: Cue for Exit,' *Sunday Times* (London) (20 February 1966), p. 12. 'Certainly dissatisfaction with the present system is widespread.'

Salem, Daniel. 'Où en est le nouveau théâtre anglais?' *Nouvelles Littéraires*, (17–23 January 1972), 24. There is a dearth of new plays in the contemporary English theatre.

Sayers, Dorothy L. 'Playwrights Are Not Evangelists,' *World Theatre*, V, no. 1 (1954), 61–6. Argues that in a world grown largely heathen, religious drama can be very powerful.

Schechner, Richard. 'Theatre Criticism,' *Tulane Drama Review*, IX, no. 3 (Spring 1965), 13–24. On interpretive criticism in today's theatre.

Scheller, Bernard. 'Zum Problem der Volksgestalten in englischsprachigen Bühnenwerken des spätbürgerlich-kritischen Realismus,' *Zeitschrift für Anglistik und Amerikanistik* (East Berlin), XXI (1973), 161–79. On the portrayal of common people in contemporary English drama.

Schneider, Alan. 'In England,' *Players Magazine*, XXIX (March 1953), 125–6. Survey.

Schoell, Edwin R. 'The Amateur Theatre in Great Britain,' *Educational Theatre Journal*, XV, no. 2 (May 1963), 151–7. 'Within its accepted limits for achievement . . . it has done an exceptional job of promoting the drama during a period of general decline.'

———. 'Theatre in the British University,' *Players Magazine*, XLI (February 1965), 124–5. 'It is indeed quite possible that the decline in the British theatre that took place in the last decade could have been averted had the stage been sufficiently supplied with intelligent and venturesome newcomers.'

Schwartz, Barry N. 'And the Wall Came Tumbling Down,' *Midwest Quarterly*, XI (1969), 83–9. On naturalism in the modern theatre.

'The Scots and the Theatre,' *Plays and Players* (London), XIII, no. 6 (March 1966), 60–1; no. 7 (April 1966), 62–3. Survey of drama in Scotland.

Scott, J. D. 'Britain's Angry Young Men,' *Saturday Review* (New York) (27 July 1957), pp. 8–11. Discusses the most controversial British literary movement of our time.

Scott, Peter Graham. 'What's Wrong with Repertory?' *Plays and Players* (London), X, no. 3 (December 1962), 23. Discusses some of the problems and the opportunities arising out of work in the regional repertory theatres.

'The Season in London,' *Theatre Arts* (New York), XXXVIII February 1954), 82–5. Survey.

'The Season's Plays Confirm the Split in London's Theatre Life,' *The Times* (London) (8 August 1962), p. 11. Survey.

Self, David. 'Edinburgh,' *Plays and Players* (London), XXI, no. 1 (October 1973), 65–6; no. 2 (November 1973), 62–3. Survey of Edinburgh Festival drama offerings.

Sellin, Eric. 'Absurdity and the Modern Theater,' *College Language Association Journal*, XII (March 1969), 199–204. Considers some of the meanings of the expression 'Theatre of the Absurd.'

Seymour, Alan. 'Theatre 1965: The National Theatre,'

London Magazine, V (August 1965), 49–54. An interview with Kenneth Tynan.

———. 'Too True, Not Good Enough,' *London Magazine*, V (December 1965), 60–4. '. . . few British writers seem successfully to have integrated the lessons of Brecht and/or Artaud.'

———. 'Fringe Winter,' *London Magazine*, XII (April–May 1972), 116–24. Survey of the winter season.

Sharon, Muriel. 'Report from England,' *Educational Theatre Journal*, V (March 1953), 20–3. On the Children's Theatre.

Shaw, Robert. 'A New English Theatre?' *London Magazine*, VII (July 1960), 30–4. An actor–dramatist talks about the state of the theatre.

Sherek, Henry. 'End or Change Stage Censorship,' *Plays and Players* (London), IX, no. 12 (September 1962), 22. Reflections.

Sherriffs, Ronald E. 'Governmental Support to the Theatre in Great Britain,' *Theatre Survey*, VI (November 1965), 91–115. General acceptance of the concept of theatre as an institution possessing positive values worthy of public support is a comparatively recent development in the history of the British theatre.

Shorey, Kenneth. 'Theater Workshop: "A British Peoples" Theater,' *Modern Age* (Chicago), V (1961), 407–12. 'If Theater Workshop is to become a valid example of popular theater to the rest of the world, then Joan Littlewood will have to re-examine her political and moral positions with relation to "the people" she professes to love and to serve.'

———. 'Contemporary Playwriting: Attempts to Regain a Popular Audience,' *Modern Age* (Chicago), VII (Spring

1963), 181–8. 'Certainly in no sense of the word can the theatre arts as they are today claim to be "communal".'

Shulman, Milton. 'Critics Are a Theatre's Best Friend,' *Plays and Players* (London), X, no. 11 (August 1963), 10–11. Draws a distinction between the academic critic and the overnight newspaper critic.

Sigal, Clancy. 'Looking Back Without Anger; Whatever Became of the Angry Young Men?' *Commonweal*, XCII (8 May 1970), 186–8. 'Slowly, as the tide receded, the "angry" artists began to disperse but not disappear.'

Simpson, Alan. 'Paddy in Shaftesbury Avenue,' *Spectator* (London), (21 December 1962), 963–4. Comparison between English and Irish theatrical tastes by an Irishman living in London.

'Situation Vacant,' *Plays and Players* (London), VIII, no. 12 (September 1961), 22. Editorial on the National Theatre.

Sladen-Smith, F. 'One-Act Plays Galore,' *Drama* (London), no. 26 (Autumn 1952), 46–9. Reviews some recently published one-act plays.

———. 'The One-Act Play Problem,' *Drama* (London), no. 30 (Autumn 1953), 48–9. Explains why so many one-act plays have recently been written.

———. 'The One-Act Play Improves,' *Drama* (London), no. 34 (Autumn 1954), 34–5. Survey of the one-act plays of the year.

Smith, Paul. 'Dublin's Lusty Theater,' *Holiday* (Philadelphia), XXXIII (April 1963), 119ff. Reflections on the Irish theatre then and now.

Smith, Warren Sylvester. 'The New Plays in London,'

Christian Century, LXXXII (1 September 1965), 1066–7; (8 September 1965), 1096–7. Survey.

Solomon, Samuel. 'The Theatre in Britain,' *Contemporary Review*, CCXII (June 1968), 326–9.

'Some Notes about the London Theater,' *Sunset*, CXV (July 1955), 8. Survey.

Sorell, Walter. 'Waiting for Godot,' *Cresset*, XXXI (September 1968), 8–15. On innovations in modern drama.

Spanos, William V. 'Modern Drama and the Aristotelian Tradition: The Formal Imperatives of Absurd Time,' *Contemporary Literature*, XII (Summer 1971), 345–72. On the rejection by the absurd drama of Aristotle's principles.

Spargur, Ronn. 'The New Drama: Starshine and Sunshine,' *Arts in Society*, VII, no. 2 (1970), 182–4. 'The new Drama, often wild and meandering in concept, is the barrel through which the moral laser streams out to knock people off crumbling foundations and carry them to new heights.'

'Spotlight on the Footlights,' *The Economist* (3 July 1954), pp. 11–13. '. . . this glittering profession, for all its frequent concomitants of disappointment and poverty, will always attract too many people.'

Spurling, Hilary. 'The Decline of the West End,' *Art in America*, LIX (May 1971), 108–9. '. . . sensations of alarm and despondency . . . have spread, this past year, throughout London's theatrical West End.'

'Stage Workshop,' *Times Literary Supplement* (London) (28 August 1959), p. 495. Editorial on the Abbey Theatre's need to create a workshop atmosphere.

Stallbaumer, Virgil. 'Modern Groundlings and the Aims of Drama,' *American Benedictine Review*, XXI (1970), 335–50. Modern drama has 'run into serious trouble on moral grounds.'

'Stark Attitudes in the West End Theatre; Tolerance in the Gallery,' *Times Literary Supplement* (9 September 1960), pp. xxxviii–xxxix.

States, Bert O. 'The Case for Plot in Modern Drama,' *Hudson Review*, XX (Spring 1967), 49–61. '. . . in the momentum of our proud revolution against the "Old" drama we have deprived ourselves of the best way of making aesthetic sense out of the strange and intractable materials of the New.'

Stein, Karen F. 'Metaphysical Silence in Absurd Drama,' *Modern Drama*, XIII (February 1971), 423–31. Includes several references to Harold Pinter and Samuel Beckett.

Strauss, George. 'National Theatre,' *New Statesman and Nation* (London), XLVI (1 August 1953), 124–5. See correspondence (8 August–26 September 1953), pp. 158, 181, 208, 234, 260, 289, 316–17, 347.

———. 'Theatre Censorship: Exit the Lord Chamberlain,' *The Times* (London) (24 September 1968), p. 9. The Labour MP discusses the Theatres Act which he introduced into the House of Commons as a Private Member's Bill.

Sudrann, Jean. 'The Necessary Illusion: A Letter from London,' *Antioch Review*, XVIII (Summer 1958), 236–44. A common theme of postwar British writers is the death of the past and the need to create a new and living identity which will be seen to be related to the past.

Sweeney, Maxwell. 'Dublin,' *Plays and Players* (London), I, no. 2 (November 1953), 24; no. 3 (December 1953), 23;

no. 5 (February 1954), 22; no. 6 (March 1954), 22. Survey.

Tarn, Adam. 'Major Dramatic Trends: 1948–1968,' *World Theatre* (UNESCO), XVII, no. 1, 2 (1969), 9–33. 'I doubt whether there has ever been in the history of the theatre such a whirlpool of ideas and of dramatic works, as in the past twenty years.'

Taylor, John Russell. 'British Drama of the Fifties,' *World Theatre*, XI, no. 3 (Autumn 1962), 241–54. Survey.

———. 'What's Happened to the New Dramatists?' *Plays and Players* (London), XI, no. 11 (August 1964), 8–9, '. . . not "new drama" any more, but just drama like any other.'

———. 'Ten Years of the English Stage Company,' *Tulane Drama Review*, XI, no. 2 (Winter 1966), 120–31. Survey.

———. 'British Dramatists: The New Arrivals,' *Plays and Players* (London), XVII, no. 7 (April 1970), 48–50, no. 8 (May 1970), 48–50, no. 9 (June 1970), 22–4, no. 10 (July 1970), 16–18, 78, no. 11 (August 1970), 16–18, no. 12 (September 1970), 12–14, 22; XVIII, no. 1 (October 1970), 14–17, no. 2 (November 1970), 16–18, 28, no. 3 (December 1970), 14–16, 26, no. 4 (January 1971), 24–8, 57, no. 5 (February 1971), 24–7, no. 6 (March 1971), 16–18. On Peter Nichols; David Mercer; David Storey; Tom Stoppard; Edward Bond; Peter Terson; Joe Orton; Charles Wood; Alan Ayckbourn and David Cregan; William Corlett, John Hopkins, Alan Plater, Cecil P. Taylor, Kevin Laffan, Christopher Hampton; Peter Barnes, Colin Spencer, David Pinner, David Halliwell, Howard Brenton, Robert Shaw and David Caute; and concluding essay, respectively.

———. 'Teach and Be Damned,' *Plays and Players* (London), XVIII, no. 12 (September 1971), 14–18. On the volume of new plays concerned with the problems of the educationalist.

———. 'What a Farce,' *Plays and Players* (London), XIX, no. 1 (October 1971), 14–16. On the new writers of farces.

'Testing Times for Dramatists,' *Times Literary Supplement* (London), Special Autumn Issue (29 August 1952), p. iv. Reflections. See Letter to the editor by C. B. Purdom (5 September 1952), p. 581.

'Theatre in Britain,' *World Theatre*, V, no. 13 (Summer 1964), 5–72. Contributions on various aspects of the theatre.

'Theatre Criticism–The Rights and the Wrongs,' *Plays and Players* (London), XIII, no. 5 (February 1966), 54–5, 67–9. Two drama critics, J. W. Lambert and Ronald Bryden, discuss contemporary theatre criticism with playwright Ann Jellicoe and director Michael Geliot.

'Theatre in Dublin,' *Dublin Magazine*, V, no. 3–4 (Autumn–Winter 1966), 3–5. Editorial. 'There is no denying that Dublin is suffering from a famine as far as the theatre is concerned.'

'Theatre 1965,' *London Magazine*, V (August 1965), 49–83. Contains: 1. Alan Seymour, 'The National Theatre;' 2. Simon Trussler, 'Theatre of Cruelty and the Failure of Liberal Humanism;' 3. Peter Hall and Jeremy Brooks, 'Royal Shakespeare Company;' 4. Philip Collins, 'Reps.;' 5. Tom Milne and Charles Marowitz, 'Argument and Augury;' 6. David Thompson, 'Stage Sixty;' 7. Arnold Wesker, 'The Round House.'

'Theatre Survey: New Authors,' *Encore* (London) (September 1958), pp. 24–39. Contributions by Ian Dallas, Irving Wardle, Stuart Hall and John Arden.

'This Sparkling Theater Season: London,' *Newsweek*, XLVI (19 December 1955), 55ff. 'Modern English theater is hardly putting its best foot forward'.

Thomas, Michael. 'At Home and Away,' *Plays and Players* (London), XIII, no. 7 (April 1966), 56–8. Investigates why so many English-speaking theater artists from abroad gravitate to London.

———. 'Buying British on Broadway,' *Plays and Players* (London), XIV, no. 4 (January 1967), 54–5. 'Broadway . . . has become more and more dependent on the West End.'

Thompson, Marjorie. 'The Image of Youth in the Contemporary Theater,' *Modern Drama*, VII, no. 4 (February 1965), 433–45. 'The younger dramatists' chief concern is young people and, in particular, their predicament in the world today.'

Thompson, William I. 'Freedom and Comedy,' *Tulane Drama Review*, IX, no. 3 (Spring 1965), 216–30. Examines the hero in the farce, the comedy and the absurd drama.

'Three at Court,' *Plays and Players* (London), XIII no. 2 (November 1965), 8–12, 50. N. F. Simpson, Ann Jellicoe and Edward Bond talk about their plays.

'Time for Action,' *Plays and Players* (London), VIII, no. 7 (April 1961), 20. Editorial on the National Theatre.

Tobin, Michael. 'The Ponderings of a Playgoer,' *Iris Hibernia* (Fribourg, Switzerland), IV, no. 3 (1960), 27–39. Remarks about the Irish theatre past and present.

'Towards a National Theatre,' *Encore* (London) (Summer 1956), pp. 13–22. A Symposium with Kenneth Tynan, Benn W. Levy, Tyrone Guthrie, Peter Hall and Flora Robson.

'Towards a Popular Theatre,' *Encore* (London) (September 1958), pp. 16–28. Contents: Michel Saint-Denis, 'New Fields of Action;' David Shepherd, 'The Search;' Arnold Wesker, 'Let Battle Commence;' Tom Milne, 'Theatre populaire actuel.'

Trelford, Donald. 'After the Chamberlain,' *Observer* (London) (25 June 1967), pp. 11–12. Considers conflicting views on stage censorship.

Trewin, J. C. 'Grand National,' *Illustrated London News*, CCXXVI (9 April 1955), 660.

———. 'A Cry of Players: The Best English Performances,' *International Theatre Annual*, II (1956–7), 183–196 Survey.

———. 'The Best Plays and Players of 1956,' *Plays and Players* (London), IV, no. 4 (January 1957), 6–7. Writes of 'the plays and players that have most impressed him during the past year.'

———. 'Bouquets, but a Few Thorns Too: English Performances of the Year,' *International Theatre Annual*, III (1957–8), 189–203. Survey.

———. 'The Best Plays and Players of 1957,' *Plays and Players* (London), V, no. 4 (January 1958), 6–7. Writes of 'the plays and players that have most impressed him during the past year.'

———. 'The Players' Festival,' *Plays and Players* (London), VI, no. 1 (October 1958), 11. Writes 'of the plays and players that most impressed him at the Edinburgh Festival last month.'

———. 'The Best Plays and Players of 1958,' *Plays and Players* (London), VI, no. 4 (January 1959), 6–7. Survey.

———. 'The Year of Revivals,' *Plays and Players* (London), VII, no. 1 (October 1959), 11. Survey of Edinburgh Festival drama productions.

———. 'The Best Plays and Players of 1959,' *Plays and Players* (London), VII, no. 4 (January 1960), 6–8. Survey.

———. 'History in the North,' *Plays and Players* (London), VIII, no. 1 (October 1960), 7, 24. Survey of Edinburgh Festival drama productions.

———. 'Fire in the North,' *Plays and Players* (London), IX, no. 1 (October 1961), 11. Survey of Edinburgh Festival drama productions.

———. 'To Call Oneself a Playgoer,' *Books*, no. 375 (1968), 124–9. What one ought to read to call oneself a playgoer.

Trilling, Ossia. 'The Young British Drama,' *Modern Drama*, III, no. 2 (September 1960), 168–77. Survey.

———. 'The New English Realism,' *Tulane Drama Review*, VII, no. 2 (Winter 1962), 184–93. The new realism can be described as a compound of two elements. 'The first represents an involuntary and instinctive resistance to the irksome class structure of British society and the other . . . the universal dilemma.'

Trussler, Simon. 'Edinburgh Drama 1964,' *Plays and Players* (London), XII, no. 1 (October 1964), 43–5. Survey of Edinburgh Theatre Festival offerings.

———. 'Cruel, Cruel London,' *Tulane Drama Review*, IX, no. 3 (Spring 1965), 207–15. On the plays of cruelty.

———. 'Theatre of Cruelty and the Failure of Liberal Humanism,' *London Magazine*, V (August 1965), 55–9. Survey.

———. 'England: The National Theatre,' *Tulane Drama Review*, X, no. 1 (Fall 1965), 148–57. Survey.

———. 'Farce,' *Plays and Players* (London), XIII, no. 9 (June 1966), 56–8, 72. '. . . farce has recently shown signs of being reinstated as a play form worthy of serious critical study.'

———. 'The London Scene,' *Tulane Drama Review*, XI, no. 4 (Summer 1967), 144–52. Survey.

———. 'Second-Generation London,' *Drama Review*, XII no. 2 (Winter 1968), 171–6. Survey.

———. 'British Neo-Naturalism,' *Drama Review*, XIII, no. 2 (Winter 1968), 130–6. Survey.

Turner, David. 'A Playwright's Position,' *Listener* (London), LXXVI (18 August 1966), 234–6. Gives his completely independent view of the problems of a television dramatist.

Turnstile, Magnus. 'Puny Critics?' *New Statesman* (London), LXXI (17 June 1966), 874–6.

Tynan, Kenneth. 'The British Stage,' *Holiday*, XIX (April 1956), 108–11, 125–8. For some time, Britain has been slowly drifting away from the serious theatre.

———. 'Cause Without a Rebel,' *Encore* (London) (June 1957), pp. 13–35. Symposium on British playwriting held at the Royal Court Theatre, 18 November 1956, with Benn W. Levy, Wolf Mankowitz, Arthur Miller, John Whiting and Colin Wilson.

———. 'The Theatre Abroad: England,' *New Yorker*, XXXV (26 September 1959), 101–25. 'A change, slight but unmistakable, has taken place.'

———. 'Some Notes on the Theater,' *American Scholar*, XXX (Winter 1960–1), 118–26. Reprinted in his book *Curtains*.

———. 'The National Theatre,' *Journal of the Royal Society of the Arts*, CXII (August 1964), 688–91.

———. 'The National Theatre,' *World Theatre*, XIII (Summer 1964), 33–6.

———. 'The National Theatre,' *Theatre*, II (1965), 75–87.

———. 'The Theatre Abroad: London,' *New Yorker*, XLIV (9 November 1968), 123–5. London is still the great place for actors.

———. 'London Is Still No. 1 in Theater, Anyway,' *Holiday*, XLVI (October 1969), 74–6, 114.

'Uncensored,' *Plays and Players* (London), VI, no. 3 (December 1958), 20. Editorial on censorship.

Ungvari, Tamas. 'A modern angol˙drama etikja,' *Vilagirodalmi Figyelo*, VIII (1962), 195–200. On the ethics of contemporary British drama.

'University Drama; A Discussion,' *New Theatre Magazine* (Bristol) (October 1959), pp. 16–20. By Susan Engel, Philip Antony, Edward Argent, Jane Howell and George Brandt.

'Up They Go,' *Plays and Players* (London), VII, no. 11 (August 1960), 20. Editorial on the necessity of 'planning' before building new theatres.

Ustinov, Peter. 'The Playwright,' *Journal of the Royal Society of Arts* (London) (2 May 1952), 415–28. One of a series of three Cantor Lectures on the modern theatre.

———. 'Some Notes on the Sticks,' *Theatre Arts* (New York), XLIII (April 1959), 14–16. Comparison between British and American theatres.

Van Heyningen, Christina. 'The Contemporary Theatre,' *Theoria*, XXXII (1969), 25–37. 'In the London theatre today one is bored to death by the way these -isms pervade nearly every play.'

Vivis, Anthony. 'Lunch & Late Night Line-Up,' *Plays and Players* (London), XVIII, no. 6 (March 1971), 52, 61. Survey of lunchtime and late-night theatres.

Vocadlo, Otakar. 'Iraka satira a divadlo,' *Svetoa Literatura*, II (1957), 76–8.

Voda-Capusan, Maria. 'Timp si anacronism in Teatrul contemporan [Time and Anachronism in the Contemporary Theatre],' *Steaua*, no. 6 (June 1969), 120–6.

Von Szeliski, John J. 'A Theatre of Possibility–and Philosophy,' *Western Humanities Review*, XXIII (Summer 1969), 249–52. 'Today's problem is that serious or "revolutionary" theatre is, in its own new ways, as greedy for sub-mental sensation as the melodramatic stage of the last century or the hokum musical of this era.'

Wain, John. 'Why Write Verse Drama?' *London Magazine*, VII (February 1960), 58–63. Review article.

Walker, Roy. 'Mermaid on the Thames,' *Theatre Arts* (New York), XLVII (March 1957), 74–6. A short history of Bernard Miles's Mermaid Theatre, established in London in 1951.

———. 'The Living Theatre,' *Critical Quarterly*, II (1960), 161–3. On the 'unfair competition with Television.'

'War Victims,' *Newsweek*, XLVIII (19 November 1956), 80. The effect of the Hungarian and Suez Canal crises.

Wardle, Irving. 'Theatre Survey: New Authors–Comedy of Menace,' *Encore* (London) (September 1958), pp. 28–33. 'The past three years have witnessed the arrival of several playwrights who have been tentatively lumped together as the "non-naturalist" or "abstractionists".'

———. 'Politics,' *International Theatre Annual*, IV (1959), 201–9. 'But amid all the talk of realism and social comment the subject of political drama has been ignored.'

———. 'Revolt Against the West End,' *Horizon*, V, no. 3 (January 1963), 26–33. 'At London's Royal Court Theatre a company of young rebels has broken with a genteel tradition in the name of defiant realism and experiment.'

———. 'Critic As Observer,' *Plays and Players* (London), X, no. 9 (June 1963), 20–1. Draws a distinction between theatre critic and theatre reviewer.

———. 'New Waves on the British Stage,' *Twentieth Century* (London), CLXXII (Summer 1963), 57–65. Reprinted in *Plays and Players* (London), XI, no. 1 (October 1963), 12–14. '. . . not only have we had a brisk turnover in idols, but also we have been entering a genuinely new climate of theatrical taste.'

———. 'Present State of the British Theatre,' *World Theatre*, XIII (Summer 1964), 5–8. Survey.

———. 'Holding Up the Mirror,' *Twentieth Century* (London), CLXXIII (Autumn 1964), 34–43. The drama critic of *The Times* tries to find out how the West End theatre in 1964 reflects the world outside it.

———. 'Farce Comes Back–or Almost,' *New Society* (26

August 1965), pp. 24–5. Farce is enjoying a spectacular boom in the British theatre.

———. 'Dramatic Criticism Today,' *Listener* (London), LXXV (21 April 1966), 584–5. '. . . drama criticism at present has no fixed base to operate from.'

———. 'A Theatre for the People,' *New Society* (19 May 1966), p. 20. 'Britain is in urgent need of a popular theatre.'

———. 'Small Theatre: Big City,' *New Society* (30 June 1966), pp. 19–20. 'the day of the old-style club theatres is over.'

———. 'London's Subsidized Companies,' *Tulane Drama Review*, XI, no. 2 (Winter 1966), 105–19.

———. 'Is There a Case for the Court?' *The Times* (London) (13 April 1968), p. 21. On censorship.

———. 'The Uncommercial Broadway,' *The Times* (London) (22 February 1969), p. 21. 'I doubt that the West End will ever be taken over as an annexe of Broadway.'

———. 'The Battleground of Youth,' *The Times* (London) (2 August 1969), p. 19. 'I suspect that if the British theatre is now moving in any clear direction it is towards the anti-theatrical young.'

———. ' "Fringe" Theatre,' *New Society* (29 June 1972), pp. 684–6. Some confusion surrounds the aims and practice of the club theatres and performance groups that have sprung up during the past four years.

Warnke, Frank J. 'Poetic Drama on European Stages,' *New Republic*, CXLI (24 August 1959), 30–1. Recent revival of poetic drama 'suggests once again the curiously limited expectations which seem to afflict Englishmen . . . when they go to the theater.'

Waterhouse, Robert. 'Edinburgh,' *Plays and Players* (London), XVI, no. 2 (November 1968), 53,59. Survey of Edinburgh Festival drama offerings.

Watts, Richard, Jr. 'Busman's Holiday in Britain,' *Theatre Arts* (New York), XLI (November 1957), 24–7. An American critic looks at the London stage.

Weales, Gerald. 'Theatre Literature and Criticism,' *Educational Theatre Journal*, XIX (June 1967), 301–7. Considers the methods and matter of criticism; the tools of the critic and their availability; and the educational implications.

———. 'Taking the Plunge: English Theater in 1970,' *North American Review*, CCLV (Winter 1970), 77–80. Survey.

Weatherby, W. J. 'Power Behind the London Stage,' *Guardian* (London) (20 January 1960), p. 6. On the Society of West End Theatre Managers.

Weaver, Robert. 'England's Angry Young Men,' *Queen's Quarterly*, LXV (Summer 1958), 183–94. The Angry Young Men 'have more social than literary significance, and most of them seem destined to be little more than an unusually noisy and pretentious group of minor writers.'

Webster, Margaret. 'The Theatre in London,' *Theatre Arts* (New York), XL (May 1956), 20–9, 84–6. The past season 'has added little lustre to British theatre history.'

———. 'A Look at the London Season,' *Theatre Arts* (New York), XLI (May 1957), 23–32, 92–4. The season has been 'a confused mass of material.'

———. 'Whither Bound?' *Theatre Arts* (New York), XLIV (November 1960), 23–4, 71. 'In England the road has given way to the "reps".'

Weightman, John. 'The Play As Fable,' *Encounter*, XXVIII (February 1967), 55–7. On the themes of homosexuality and alienation in contemporary British drama.

Wellwarth, George. 'Theater in London,' *Modern Drama*, II, no. 1 (May 1959), 47–50. Survey.

Wesker, Arnold. 'How To Cope With Criticism,' *Plays and Players* (London), XX, no. 3 (December 1972), 18–19. Underlines the dangers to drama in the vanity of critics.

'What's Wrong With the Abbey?' *Plays and Players* (London), X, no. 5 (February 1963), 22–4. Views of director Hilton Edwards, dramatist Hugh Leonard, manager Phyllis Ryan and critic Maurice Kennedy.

Whitaker, Thomas R. 'Notes on Playing the Player,' *Centennial Review* (Michigan State University), XVI (1972), 1–22. Tries to find out whether modern drama has 'any real unity, any major direction.'

Whiting, John. 'A Writer's Prospect—V. The Writers' Theatre,' *London Magazine*, III, no. 12 (1956), 48–52. 'The performance of a play cannot be arrived at without a hundred compromises on the part of the writer'.

———. 'The Masses Is Too Stupid for Us,' *London Magazine*, VII (July 1960), 34–7. Review article.

———. 'The Popular Theatre,' *London Magazine*, I (February 1962), 84–7. 'Conservatism is the life-blood of the popular theatre: radicalism its death.'

Whitworth, Robin. 'Do We Need a National Theatre?' *Drama* (London), no. 54 (Autumn 1959), 38–40. The Deputy

Chairman of the British Drama League and Member of the Joint Council of the National Theatre and Old Vic talks about the latest developments in the National Theatre Scheme.

'Why the Subsidized Theatres Resent Criticism,' *The Times* (London) (4 July 1966), p. 14. '. . . with belligerent posters in the Royal Court foyer, protest meetings, and the Osborne campaign, it looks as though Mr. Peter Hall's often quoted slogan, "the right to fail", denies outsiders the right to detect any failure.'

Wickham, Glynne. 'Universities and the Theatre,' *Encore* (London) (May–June 1958), pp. 13–17. The Principal of the Drama Department of Bristol University discusses British Universities' attitude towards Drama as a subject.

———. 'The Study of Drama in the British Universities, 1945–1966,' *Theatre Notebook*, XXI, no. 1 (1966), 15–20.

Wicks, Helen. 'Fun at the Festival,' *Plays and Players* (London), VII, no. 11 (August 1960), 6–7. Preview of Edinburgh Festival drama offerings.

Williams, Alan Vaughan, 'Rep–After the Hand-Out,' *Plays and Players* (London), XIII, no. 11 (August 1966), 52–3. On the implications latent in the increased grants to repertory theatres.

Williams, Raymond. 'Drama and the Left,' *Encore* (London) (March 1959), pp. 6–12. Believes that a major difficulty is that the majority theatre in England has been for some time a predominantly middle-class institution.

———. 'New English Drama,' *Twentieth Century*, CLXX (Autumn 1961), pp. 169–80. '. . . a period of extreme confusion and eclecticism.' Reprinted, in a revised form, in *The Modern Age*, The Pelican Guide to English Literature

7, ed. Boris Ford (Harmondsworth, Middlesex: Penguin Books, 1961), pp. 496–508.

———. 'Strindberg and the New Drama in Britain,' *World Theatre*, XI, no. 1 (Spring 1962), 61–6.

Williamson, Audrey. 'No Lack of Dramatists,' *Drama* (London), no. 49 (Summer 1958), 32–5. On the new playwrights.

Willis, Lord. 'Is Theatre Censorship Necessary?' *Listener* (London), LXXV (26 May 1966), 749–50. 'As an institution it ought to go.'

Willis, Ted. 'TV and the Dramatist,' *Plays and Players* (London), XII, no. 9 (June 1965), 19, 50. A comparison between TV and stage drama.

Wilmeth, Don B. 'The Latest Decade of Theatre: Death or Deliverance?' *Choice*, VIII (February 1972), 1557–62. A bibliographical article.

Wilmot, Seamus. 'The Gaelic Theatre,' *Éire-Ireland*, III (Summer 1968), 63–71. Survey of the drama in the Irish language.

Wilson, Angus. 'New Playwrights,' *Partisan Review*, XXVI (Fall 1959), 631–4.

Worsley, T. C. 'The Task of the Dramatic Critic,' *Listener* (London) (12 November 1953), pp. 810–12. 'What is required of the critic . . . is that he should not lag behind the rest of the theatre-going public, that he should lead and not merely follow.'

———. 'Off with the Old,' *New Statesman and Nation* (London), XLVII (2 January 1954), 12. Survey.

———. 'The National Theatre,' *New Statesman and Nation*

(London), LI (4 February 1956), 123. See correspondence, LI (11 February 1956), 154; (10 March 1956), 214.

———. 'A New Wave Rules Britannia,' *Theatre Arts* (New York), XLV (October 1961), 17–19. '. . . the postwar social revolution has produced a young generation of playwrights who are class-conscious only to a point, but gifted in great measure.'

———. 'Don't Be Beastly to the Critics,' *Plays and Players* (London), X, no. 4 (January 1963), 20–1. On the responsibilities of the drama critic.

Wrede, Casper. 'New Wine into Old Bottles,' *London Magazine*, VII (July 1960), 37–9. Discussion of the state of the theatre.

Wright, David. 'In Search of an Audience,' *Plays and Players* (London), XIII, no. 10 (July 1966), 66–7. Talks to Michael Geliot, Frank Dunlop and Michael Kustow.

———. 'Documentary Theatre,' *Plays and Players* (London), XIV, no. 2 (November 1966), 60–1. On the background to a currently fashionable label.

Young, Elizabeth. 'Cause Without Effect,' *Reporter*, XX (30 April 1959), 36–7. '. . . the British theater is definitely back among the art forms and no longer a vehicle for a cause.'

Zinsser, William K. 'The Vanishing Boffola,' *Horizon*, III (January 1961), 122–3. 'A creaky set of English comics keeps alive the fun that is gone from the American stage.'